D1117363

Reinventing Government
or Reinventing Ourselves

SUNY Series in Public Administration
Peter W. Colby, Editor

Reinventing Government
or Reinventing Ourselves

The Role of Citizen Owners
in Making a Better Government

Hindy Lauer Schachter

State University of New York Press

Published by
State University of New York Press, Albany

© 1997 State University of New York

For information, address State University of New York
Press, State University Plaza, Albany, N.Y., 12246

Production by Diane Ganeles
Marketing by Fran Keneston

Library of Congress Cataloging-in-Publication Data

Schachter, Hindy Lauer.
    Reinventing government or reinventing ourselves : the role of citizen
owners in making a better government / Hindy Lauer Schachter.
        p.   cm. — (SUNY series in public administration)
    Includes bibliographical references (p.   ) and index.
    ISBN 0–7914–3155–X (hb. : alk. paper). — ISBN 0–7914–3156–8
(pkb. : alk. paper)
        1. Political participation—United States.   2. Administrative agencies—
United States—Reorganization.   3. Administrative agencies—United
States—Management.   4. Government publicity—United States.
5. Public administration—United States—History.   6. Bureau of Municipal
Research (New York, N.Y.)—History.   I. Title.   II. Series.
JK1764.S35 **1997**
353.07'5—dc20   96–12019
                                                                                    CIP

10 9 8 7 6 5 4 3 2 1

*As always
to
Irving and Amanda
and now also to
Alex*

CONTENTS

Acknowledgments
ix

1. Two Models of Reform
1

2. The Bureau of Municipal Research
17

3. Citizens as Owners
31

4. Controversy over the Schools
43

5. Analysis
55

6. Strategies for Reform
77

Notes
93

References
119

Index
135

ACKNOWLEDGMENTS

I could not have written this book without assistance. A Fall 1994 sabbatical from New Jersey Institute of Technology made research at Columbia University's Oral History and Manuscript Collections, the Institute of Public Administration's library, and the Rockefeller Archive Center possible. I enjoyed working with all three institutions' archivists, but I want to single out Erwin Levold of the Rockefeller Archive Center in Pocantico Hills, North Tarrytown, New York for first-rate professional help.

Some of the material in chapters 3 and 5 originally appeared as "Reinventing Government or Reinventing Ourselves: Two Models for Improving Government Performance," *Public Administration Review* vol. 55, no. 6 (1995). I thank David Rosenbloom, editor of *Public Administration Review*, for encouraging me to refine my arguments. His interest was one factor propelling me to create this book.

Some of the material in chapter 4 originally appeared in "Democracy, Scientific Management and Urban Reform: The Case of the Bureau of Municipal Research and the 1912 New York City School Inquiry," *Journal of Management History*, vol. 1, no. 2 (1995). The article was part of a symposium I edited on the impact of scientific management on public administration. I thank Jack Rabin, the journal's editor, for suggesting that I edit the symposium. I am grateful for my conversations with Chris Nyland, University of Wollongang, Australia, on the interfaces among democracy, scientific management, and urban reform. I thank James Stever for his comments.

Clay Morgan has performed well as my editor at SUNY Press. I thank Diane Ganeles for serving as production editor for the manuscript. My final and most heartfelt thanks go to my husband Irving and my daughter Amanda.

CHAPTER 1

TWO
MODELS
OF REFORM

This book attempts to unite a call for active citizenship to the current concern for improving public-agency performance. The method is to analyze a turn-of-the century model of urban reform that depicts the public as owners of its government rather than as customers, the metaphor popular in contemporary reform proposals, and to show how this strong-citizen model leads to the conclusion that establishing an active public is essential to increasing agency efficiency and responsiveness. Active citizenship is defined as people engaged in deliberation to influence public-sector decision-making, animated, at least in part, by concern for the public interest, a concept that each individual may define in a different way. Active citizens shape the political agenda; they deliberate on the ends that governments should pursue as well as evaluating how well particular public-sector programs work now.

We live in a time of great clamor for better agency service. Practitioners and academics discuss reform proposals under the rubric "reinventing government," an apt title because they assume producing a government that works better and costs less comes from structural and procedural change within the government itself.[1] When managers shift rules, the desirable outcomes of government increase without getting into messy questions of politics which are said to only intensify the problem because "[I]n Washington's highly politicized world, the greatest risk is not that a program will perform poorly, but that a scandal will erupt."[2]

1

The focus of this reform literature is on how government should work rather than on what it should do. Attempts are made to streamline agencies, privatize programs and relax civil-service procedures and procurement rules. Few people consider the idea that no matter how government structures its tasks or changes its rules and procedures, neither efficiency nor responsiveness will increase significantly until citizens shift their orientation, accept an owner's role and participate in the public sphere, contributing their ideas to improve problem solving. In other words few people question the dictum that reform efforts should center unilaterally on reinventing government rather than also on reinventing citizenship with more stress on the "average" American's participation in public-sector agenda setting.

As a field of inquiry, public administration is no stranger to attempts to increase agency performance. Its emergence as a pragmatic, action-oriented field at the turn-of-the-century was based on a union of the urban reform and scientific management movements both of which envisioned government that would work better and cost less. Throughout the century key members of the public-administration community moved back and forth between academe and federal commissions applying their knowledge to reinvigorate government agencies. Members of the then embryonic public-administration community participated in President Taft's 1912 Commission on Economy and Efficiency, an early federal task force positing that organizational and procedural changes would enhance efficiency.[3] They were key players on President Franklin Roosevelt's 1937 Committee on Administrative Management which concluded that efficiency canons required establishing a responsible chief executive with adequate staff support.[4] Their role has been less significant, however, in some of the federal government's most recent endeavors such as the 1982 Grace Commission and Vice President Gore's National Performance Review Task Force.

The argument of this book is that public administration in its early years took a broader approach to the prerequisites for increasing agency efficiency than is fashionable in the contemporary reinventing government proposals. At least some part of the early public-administration literature saw increased performance as dependent on citizen renewal as well as on internal structural and procedural change. Writers proffered two approaches to increased efficiency, one primarily managerial and the other political. The first is generally discussed under the rubric of "public-administration principles"; the second can be called a literature on the treatment of agency stakeholders. The first literature addresses managers; the second seeks a lay audience and concerns itself with its obligations. This explicitly political literature assumes that reinventing government is a necessary but insufficient condition for genuine reform. A more efficient government also requires reinventing ourselves, especially our orientation to the public sphere. Citizens must learn to take a greater interest in their communities and become more involved in monitoring governmental performance. Citizen action is essential to creating government that works better whether or not it costs less. Let us briefly examine each literature in turn.

The Principles and Stakeholder Approaches

The first literature, which stretches from Frederick Taylor to Luther Gulick and Lyndall Urwick (roughly from 1895 to 1937) examines the internal mechanisms of public and private organizations with an eye towards establishing principles to increase output/input. It begins with Taylor's exhortation that management should "rest upon well recognized, clearly defined and fixed principles instead of depending upon more or less hazy ideas received from a limited observation."[5] It makes references to work by people such as Harrington Emerson and Henri Fayol who were primarily concerned with elucidating principles of private-sector efficiency but whose organizational dicta were also seen as applicable to the public sector.[6] (Emerson took his twelve principles of efficiency with him when he became an efficiency advisor to the socialist government of Milwaukee.)[7] Its widely recognized zenith is a collection of essays edited by Gulick and Urwick in 1937, *Papers on the Science of Administration*.[8]

The second approach, pioneered by turn-of-the-century political Progressives, focuses exclusively on the public sector and on ways to improve efficiency by strengthening the links between bureaucrats and their stakeholders. This literature is also indebted to Taylor but in relation to his methodological belief that administrative problems were researchable and that improvements could come from comparisons and experimentation. Key participants in this literature associated with New York's Bureau of Municipal Research (BMR) coined a concept of "efficient citizenship" which posited that urban citizens owned their government and as owners had a duty to get involved in city affairs, help organized bureaus get information on political/administrative performance and instruct politicians and bureaucrats in shareholder demands for improvement. The bureau argued that efficiency required both efficient organizations and efficient citizens.[9] (As we will see in chapter 2, the bureau used an expansive concept of efficiency that tied the word to responsiveness rather than simply to output/input or least-cost.)

During 1907–1914 and shortly afterwards, the phrase efficient citizenship became a buzzword of sorts among people concerned with improving municipal politics. In 1913 an organization working to attract more urban investment borrowed the phrase for its own newsletter extolling the virtues of active citizen-owners.[10] A 1915 city-government text cites bureau work as its source for the observation that the

> first essential of efficient administration is intelligent citizenship. In most discussions of municipal reform this is put last on the list, as if it were merely a by-product of charter overhauling . . . That is getting at things from the wrong angle altogether . . . The citizen can no more throw all his civic responsibilities upon experts than the churchman can shift his quest for salvation upon the clergy.[11]

Another textbook cites the bureau in connection with the hypothesis that

> [I]n our effort to improve municipal service, we have been emphasizing too much the responsibility of the public official, and thinking too little about the responsibility of the citizen . . . Good city government can be as severely handicapped through indifferent citizenship as through apathetic administration.[12]

Articles by municipal reformers also discuss this aspect of the bureau's work.[13]

The fate of these two approaches to change has been very different. The principles literature is generally considered the originating paradigm of the field. Few modern public-administration students read principles works in their entirety but everyone in the community knows they exist and has at least some idea of their fundamental content. Widely-used introductory textbooks, case compendia, and excerpts from historical readings cite Taylor and the essays compiled by Gulick and Urwick.[14]

Participants in undergraduate and Master of Public Administration (MPA) programs learn about the structural recommendations proffered in Gulick and Urwick's *Papers on the Science of Administration*. Students are told that the articles in this compilation are a foundation on which the edifice of public administration as a field of inquiry rests. The basic concepts of *Papers on the Science of Administration* become part of their vocabulary. Most learn that the principles literature posits that organizational specialization or division of labor increases efficiency, authority should be commensurate with responsibility, unity of command is crucial, the manager should have a relatively tight span of control.

Of course they do not imbibe this material in a time warp. Along with the classic pre-war concepts, they read excerpts from later authors such as Herbert Simon[15], which are meant to convince them that an overreliance on the immutability of principles is a scholarly and practical dead end. The principles literature offers to tell practicing managers how to maximize output/input, and Simon argues that the advice is not very useful on a case-by-case basis. Specialization is a key precept in the principles literature but the manager's problem is not simply whether to specialize but how to decide the basis for dividing labor. Simon points out that the principles literature does not explain whether geographical or functional division works best in a particular situation—and this type of case-by-case prescription is what the practicing manager wants from a set of dicta.

Simon points out that if unity of command means that only one person can give orders to a given worker, then this principle is incompatible with specialization because a worker may need advice from different experts. The classical literature leaves managers with a choice between following either of two important principles with no guide as to when they should choose unity of command and when they need specialization by functional expertise.

Simon also notes that tight span of control conflicts with keeping the number of hierarchical layers to a minimum. For large organizations, narrow spans of control lead to excessive red tape, for many decisions have to move up and down among multiple levels which is cumbersome and time consuming. After reading Simon, students do not necessarily forego the principles but they learn to take a more tentative approach to structural questions.

Many students also investigate Vincent Ostrom's somewhat controversial challenge to what he considers the classical theory's unfortunate monocentricity, its axiom that a single center of power will dominate any government and its ensuing preference not to fragment authority, proliferate agencies or duplicate services.[16] Ostrom calls for a theory of democratic administration characterized by polycentricity where people have access to alternative public-sector forums for service provision. His alternative has a bottom-up and heterogeneous character lacking in classical theory. His purpose in citing the pre-war literature (e.g., Gulick and Urwick) is to supercede it but in so doing he keeps alive the tenor of the classical arguments if only as a target for his own vision. The MPA student who reads Ostrom must learn something about Gulick.

Practitioners seeking to reinvent government also grapple with the principles literature. Vice President Al Gore's National Performance Review report finds it problematic that current bureaucratic structures and procedures follow a 1930s paradigm stressing large, top down, centralized agencies with rigid hierarchies in which tasks are broken into simple parts each defined by myriad rules. In an earlier day such arrangements stressing specialization and unity of command may have made sense but in today's world they do not work very well.[17]

Reinventing government challenges the legacy of the principles era. Gore cites Taylor's work only to conclude that "these approaches now seem to limit productivity rather than promote it . . . Taylor's theories about "scientific management" are no longer applicable in the information age."[18] [The relationship between the principles and the Gore report is reminiscent of an early Heinrich Boll story where the protagonist lands a steady job and achieves an identity of sorts by joining a vaudeville act and becoming the man at whom the knives are thrown.[19] The principles literature has a permanent job as the constellation of ideas against which later writers rebel; it is the metaphorical man at whom the knives are thrown.]

In contrast the efficient citizenship concept has vanished from both academic and practitioner vocabularies. Textbooks may devote one or two sentences to the Bureau of Municipal Research as one of the founders of the scientific study of public administration but no widely used introductory text explains that the bureau stressed the essential role of a committed citizenry in improving agency performance. Jane Dahlberg's history of the bureau barely mentions efficient citizenship.[20] The organization's place in public-administration history is built on its budgetary and structural work.[21] The lack of any modern analysis of the bureau's citizen-owner concept leads some commentators to classify the BMR as an apolitical, technocratic organization.[22]

This skewed picture of the bureau is problematic because the efficient citizenship concept offers an alternative to the citizen-as-customer metaphor that is so central to the current reinventing government scenario. David Osborne and Ted Gaebler's *Reinventing Government*, the book that gave 1990s reform impetus, insists that the path to change lies through customer-driven government.[23] Agencies must learn to meet the needs of their customers even though few public-sector organizations historically used that term in thinking about the people with whom they dealt.

In Vice President Gore's National Performance Review, the customer metaphor pops up everywhere. The report opens with the announcement that the linchpin for reform is "a new customer service contract with the American people."[24] Administrators are to give citizens the same responsiveness and consideration businesses supposedly give customers. Each agency will have customer-service plans that train public administrators in customer-service skills. These plans will list businesses with which agencies should compare themselves on this crucial dimension so that they can become equal to the best that the private sector has to offer. Customer satisfaction will become a prime criterion in evaluating agency managers and employees.[25] An entire chapter is entitled "Putting Customers First."

The customer metaphor crops up in local attempts at reform as well. The International City/County Management Association's latest guide to effective communication tells local agency managers that the customer orientation provides one of the most useful ways of understanding citizens.[26] When IBM's chief executive officer co-authored a book on reinventing schools, he used the customer model to argue against a political approach to school control. Agreeing with the dangers articulated by the National Performance Review, he feared the affect of politics on service provision. Favoring a minimal role for elected school boards, he championed an economic model of schooling which would bring together customers (parents and children) and sellers (the school administrators) and spur improvements.[27] A major influence on all these works is an innovative industrial approach to managing quality called Total Quality Management (TQM) with its notion that the organization's first duty is to delight and satisfy customers. TQM posits that to excel companies must ask themselves: Who are your customers and what are their needs?[28]

The use of a particular metaphor to comprehend political reality is much more than a linguistic conceit. By helping people understand one thing in terms of another, figurative analogies organize thinking patterns. Each metaphor highlights some aspects of the concept to be known and deflects attention away from other aspects.[29] When hermeneutical analysis compares architectural monuments to texts, social scientists accept the metaphor even though they know differences exist between buildings and written documents. The analogy is useful because it helps researchers conceptualize that the meanings embedded in stone constructions can be probed with some of the tools designed for document analysis.[30] On the other hand, Harlan Cleveland urges social scientists not to use metaphors from physics to describe information; in his view, analogies between data and energy lead to misunderstandings by emphasizing that information is similar to other resources which are, in fact, nonrenewable while information will not dissipate through use.[31]

A metaphor that equates citizens with customers gives one perspective from which to gauge society's needs for performance improvement. Shifting the metaphor can point the way to a focus on overlooked aspects of reality and the consideration of fresh alternatives. A new figure of speech is likely to spark new assumptions about public governance.

George Frederickson was one of the first to critique the customer-centered model for using an inappropriate metaphor.[32] He argues that citizens are not the customers of government; they represent its owners who elect leaders to represent their interests. A customer-centered model puts citizens in a reactive role where they are limited to liking or disliking services and hoping that the administrators will change delivery if enough customers object. Owners play a proactive role; they decide what the government's agenda will be.

Before the public-administration community accepts a customer-centered model it would be useful to compare it with a model of citizenship that stresses ownership. Looking at such a model does not address all of the problems that have been raised in relation to reinventing government. Another type of analysis would be needed to explore whether the reinventing government scenario thwarts legislative control of policy making by allowing agencies to unilaterally decide how to satisfy customers.[33]

The customer-owner comparison does allow seeing if a different way of looking at citizen roles leads to new emphasis on the changes that are necessary to improve government performance. It addresses the following questions: Should reform center almost exclusively on trying to change structure or will all attempts to significantly improve efficiency and responsiveness fail without a reinvigorated citizenry? Should we target proposals for change exclusively to the agencies (who will know how to help their customers) or should we also try to change the ways we socialize the population at large so that citizens are more likely to accept a conscious role as owners of the public enterprise? What proposals for change would it make sense to target to the public at large to help reinvigorate their role?

Unfortunately, the major contemporary reform prescriptions tend not to elaborate owner metaphors.[34] This lacuna in the modern literature is one reason exploring the Bureau of Municipal Research's work is useful for critiquing reinventing government. Comparing the much debated customer model with the bureau's idea of citizen-owners shows that the earlier concept provided a much more expansive public role. It envisioned citizens who were active rather than passive; it tried to foster a public that possessed a concern for communal needs rather than a conglomerate of individualistic consumers, each with a monochromatic interest in fulfilling his or her own individual desires. The efficient citizenship model not only posited the necessity of supporting an enhanced public role, it also identified strategies for producing citizens who would want to act like owners. Studying this model provides one path for uniting a call to active citizenship with a concern for better government.

Efficient Citizenship: Rise and Fall

Although the concept of efficient citizenship has vanished from the contemporary public-administration dialogue, it was once an acknowledged signpost for the more radical proponents of urban reform. People using the term insisted that genuine reform entailed managerial (structural/procedural) and political (stakeholder) change.

Between its 1907 incorporation and 1914, calls for an active citizenry were a key part of the Bureau of Municipal Research's work. That efficient citizenship played a seminal role on the organization's agenda emerges clearly from studying the writings of the bureau's founders and analyzing the organization's miscellaneous publications which appeared under the heading, *Efficient Citizenship*.

Let us imagine a person who knows nothing about contemporary public-administration textbooks and has before himself or herself articles from 1914. A natural assumption would be that modern authors would treat the efficient citizenship concept in similar fashion to the principles literature. The concept would be challenged and in certain respects supplanted by later work but public-administration students would learn something about its contours. That this pattern of discussion and amendment has not been fulfilled, that the efficient citizenship concept lost all place in public discourse requires explanation. In this case the explanation is thoroughly political. The concept was discarded because it pulled the organization in a direction that was too radical for a prominent donor. As the narrative will show, examining the politics of this concept's demise is important for understanding the practical implications of active citizenship; the story of the model's fall helps to pinpoint the type of enemies the notion of citizen-owners can produce.

Efficient Citizenship and Extrinsic Influences

An analysis of efficient citizenship's rise and fall requires answering certain questions in the sociology of inquiry. These questions include: Why do academics and practitioners stop using a concept in the absence of specific empirical justification for dropping it? Do people in a field simply forget about or disregard certain concepts that were important to their predecessors or do formal and informal incentive systems exist that make it politic not to mention idea X or hypothesis Y at certain times? Who gets to choose which ideas are kept at the front of discourse?

Philosopher of science Stephen Toulmin argues that an intellectual community develops on three levels: the discipline (the ideas themselves); the institutions through which the ideas are transmitted; and the individuals who develop and transmit the ideas.[35] Textbooks trying to chart the history of public administration as a scholarly enterprise concentrate on the first level; they record objective shifts in ideas between eras (e.g., they will tell students that early writers believed in small spans of control; modern authors tend to favor different spans depending on the environment). Very little attention is given to social context—to the extradisciplinary agendas of the people and the institutions that develop ideas and how extradisciplinary prioritizing affects scholarly discourse. Little is made of the way that the social atmosphere influences change in ideas or of the social negotiation skills that writers need to understand which ideas are likely to gain a positive reception in the various communities with which they interact.

An analysis geared to include all three of Toulmin's levels would explore ideas in a social milieu where people have numerous intellectual and nonintellectual reasons for accepting or rejecting concepts. Rationales would include how acceptance/rejection affects a person's ability to meet his or her own needs and the organization's ability to sustain its entire agenda. This type of analysis would show how social evaluation influences interpretation and acceptance of specific knowledge claims.

A field of inquiry's ideas can rise or fall for *intrinsic* (i.e., intellectual) or *extrinsic* reasons.[36] In the first case, people transmitting a concept realize that it cannot explain the phenomenon under study. In the second case analysts perceive that rewards to their own careers are not forthcoming when they embrace concept X.

Accepting the importance of the extrinsic dimension means highlighting the social context within which ideas are produced. Social context in turn has internal and external dimensions.

The internal dimension relates to incentives offered within the field of inquiry itself and often manifests itself in academic politics and infighting. Neophytes who want to learn a discipline spend at least several years exploring a body of established knowledge. Inevitably they acquire personalized preconceptions about which approaches to problem solving are most likely to bring rewards from people highly placed in the field. After this socialization they may believe they have little to gain from treading in waters held in low esteem by a mentor even if they are convinced those waters hold interesting and viable knowledge paths. They drop a concept not because they see its logical flaws but rather because they do not discern that using it will help their careers.

The external dimension relates to incentives offered by sources outside the discipline, a major issue being the impact of donors. Research and writing often require outside support from organizations or individuals who stipulate that they will only fund certain kinds of projects. Consciously or unconsciously writers may steer their proposals in directions favored by sources proffering support. Other ideas are not pursued even though they may be equally useful for expanding the discipline's boundaries.

In one of the few analyses to examine the impact of funding on the development of public administration as a field of inquiry, Alasdair Roberts shows that the Rockefeller philanthropies contributed to entrenching the often criticized politics/administration dichotomy. He argues that the expansion of the public-administration community between 1927 and 1936 was dependent on funding from Rockefeller philanthropies that were sensitive to public complaints about their involvement in politics; the politics/administration dichotomy was a rhetorical device to deflect such criticism and allow the foundations to support administrative projects.[37]

Roberts notes that the American public distrusted John Rockefeller and the power he might wield through his charitable giving. Rockefeller failed to get a national charter for his Rockefeller Foundation when he tried in 1909 and only received a New York State charter in 1913.[38] These setbacks made him leery of sparking controversy by supporting advocacy work on contentious questions. The year 1914 was a particularly bad time for his public reputation; in April of that year the infamous Ludlow Massacre occured where guards murdered families of striking workers at a Rockefeller controlled company in Colorado.

What Roberts does not explain is how well placed was public distrust of the power his charitable giving might bring. Prior to the 1920s the Rockefeller interests did use their wealth to punish organizations that differed with them on political issues. Rockefeller functionaries—using the family's money as a club—were willing and able to tell writers in the public-administration community how to structure their approach to reform—which concepts to stress and which to discard with an eye to limiting approaches that stressed popular participation over the role of experts.

The argument of this book is that pressure from the Rockefeller philanthropies killed efficient citizenship as a major item on the BMR agenda. The concept was a key part of the organization's approach to reform before 1914 and virtually absent afterwards. The bureau restructured in 1914 under pressure from the Rockefellers and eliminated as an organizational player the one individual who insisted that the original vision on citizen participation had to remain intact.

Efficient citizenship did not succumb as a component of reform principally because it showed intellectual weaknesses. Philosophical and practical objections can be leveled against the citizen-owner concept; as the book shows later both the customer and owner metaphor are logically flawed. But intellectual argument did not kill efficient citizenship. This exciting, innovative idea was pushed out as too radical and inflammatory by opponents who wielded money rather than logical analysis as their weapon of choice. That other writers did not take the concept up after the BMR discarded it could be tied, at least partly, to the public-administration community as a whole depending on Rockefeller funding throughout the 1920s and 1930s. As Alasdair Roberts notes, "No important part of the public administration community was untouched by the (Rockefeller) philanthropies."[39]

Public administration has suffered from this demise. From the turn-of-the-century to our own time the field has enjoyed a rich, uninterrupted history of debating agency structures both from the perspective of recording actual patterns and searching for improvements. This intergenerational legacy has produced a sophisticated literature on organization theory.

No comparable literature on active citizenship exists. Stirring cries for more participation come from political philosophers. Some of them celebrate the Greek conception of the polis as the sphere of freedom.[40] Hannah Arendt relates that Americans of the revolutionary period knew that public freedom meant having a share in the public business; late eighteenth-century Americans did not consider public participation a burden but rather a source of happiness that they could receive nowhere else.[41] Benjamin Barber celebrates strong democracy which he conceives of as politics in the participatory mode with citizens subjecting conflicts of interest to "a never-ending process of deliberation, decision and action."[42] But these philosophers do not link their proposals to concrete issues of agency improvement. When Frederickson argues that citizens are agency owners rather than customers he cannot refer to a long list of public-administration works that explicate the importance of the different metaphors. A person who wanted to present efficient citizenship as a challenge to reinventing government would have to go back and read the original Bureau sources to understand their underlying insights. Such reading in historical sources is the central strategy behind this book which investigates a long moribund concept as a springboard for reconstructing an owner-citizen role and seeing how it influences change proposals. A key rationale for the historical exploration is that the public-administration community should understand the implications of both customer and owner metaphors before it chooses either as its guide to administrative reform.

This analysis provides a good example of how historical ideas can illuminate modern issues by throwing a different shade of light on them. Examining the Bureau's work shows what can be lost by neglecting old ideas—a loss that is poignant even though most modern readers are likely to find the older literature somewhat naive in its authors' expectations from the average citizen.

The point of exploring the model is not to sell it in toto to a contemporary audience but rather to show a different insight on the relationship between citizens and administrators and how this point of view might contribute to improving governmental performance. In addition by showing how the concept of efficient citizenship was eliminated the book contributes to exploring the role of extra-intellectual forces (particularly money) in determining which ideas receive publicity and become central to the community's discourse. As the analysis will show the bureau's administrators were somewhat naive about the affect of money on the progression of ideas. Discussing the role of funding agents in setting intellectual agendas may prevent the modern public-administration community from succumbing to the same naivete.

Several analyses of turn-of-the-century Progressivism suggest it was a middle-class movement that tried to diminish the political role of the poor.[43] Because the bureau is associated with the Progressive cause, some people may think it perverse to use the concept of efficient citizenship to argue for a more expansive citizen role. It is therefore important to realize that in the 1906–1914 era, bureau leaders often took political stands that opposed what the modern public-administration community considers typical Progressive reforms when these changes substituted elite decision making for policy determined through normal municipal channels. The bureau insisted that decisions about urban utilities and transportation should be made through city elections rather than by state public-service commissions.[44] It favored large, heterogeneous, activist big-city school boards appointed by the mayor rather than small, elite boards that delegated extensively to professional superintendents.[45]

Although, in practice, middle-class people were the prime audience for the bureau's message (as they are the primary audience for books on reinventing government), the BMR writers intended the owner metaphor to apply to every citizen—rich or poor, WASP or ethnic, male or female.[46] In this book the concept is investigated in the expansive mood in which it was conceived.

The book is divided into two parts. The first is historical in nature, examining the development of the efficient citizenship concept and its reception in its own era. Chapter 2 describes the formation of the Bureau of Municipal Research and lists some of its accomplishments. Chapter 3 explores the genesis and implications of the efficient citizenship concept. Chapter 4 analyzes a controversy about school governance that engulfed the bureau beginning in 1911; it demonstrates the concrete, political positions that the efficient citizenship doctrine led the organization to take and the enmity this approach spawned in people advocating a more restricted citizen role. Sometimes a philosophy's essence emerges most clearly through the type of enemies it attracts; the case study shows clearly the difficulties efficient citizenship poses for people who want experts controlling the public agenda.

The second part of the book relates the efficient citizenship idea to current attempts to reinvent government. Chapter 5 compares customer and owner metaphors and shows the active, community-centered nature of the latter; it analyzes how the BMR's owner metaphor shifts the locus of action from the agency to the public. This chapter also looks at the vexing question of whether it is realistic to expect modern citizens to adopt an owner's orientation. It concludes that we cannot expect to counter widespread alienation without first changing the way society educates people to assume a citizen's role and provides them with usable information on public affairs.

The last chapter offers two strategies for moving towards a polity in which citizens can assume an owner's stance. The first strategy centers on education and builds on the concept of service learning. The second proposes that cities treat citizens at least as well as corporations treat shareholders and produce a user-friendly annual report that is mailed to all households. Both are set on a foundation of ideas that the bureau advocated before 1914.

CHAPTER 2

THE BUREAU OF
MUNICIPAL RESEARCH

The Bureau of Municipal Research was an offshoot of the nine-teenth-century urban-reform movement whose middle-class and professional protagonists sought to eradicate what they saw as the corrupt and inefficient government produced by bosses and party machines.[1] The BMR emerged as the movement was shifting from recommending "government by the good" (under the assumption that throwing out the rascals would improve performance) to trying to change governmental structures to induce "government by the efficient."[2] The bureau accelerated this trend as the first organization to use Frederick Taylor's shop management insights to help solve urban problems. The organization's agenda represents the premier attempt to deliberately compare city work techniques to help agencies perform their tasks more expeditiously.[3] The bureau's administrators believed that bringing scientific management to city work would increase the data that citizens needed to supervise public administrators and make "democracy a living, vital thing."[4]

The man primarily responsible for the organization's genesis, William Henry Allen, was born in Leroy, Minnesota (population 300) in 1874.[5] He served as a teacher in the ungraded school at nearby Wykoff before continuing his education at the University of Chicago (AB 1897). The University of Pennsylvania awarded him a 1900 economics PhD for a dissertation on sanitary administration.

After receiving his doctorate, Allen chose social work as the field for his talents. His first position was as a field agent with the New Jersey State Charities Aid Association where he monitored alms houses and insane asylums. In later years Allen said that he noticed immediately that those institutions which kept accurate records tended to be clean and have relatively humane practices.[6] He also saw that formal education had not prepared him for all the vagaries of field work where "You couldn't get answers out of books."[7] Often he encountered a problem in the field only to realize that neither the literature he had read at school nor on his own covered the real-world situations encountered among the poor and institutionalized.[8] These unexpected occurrences alerted him to information's crucial role in helping administrators perform their functions and the need for an experiential component to professional education.

In 1903 Allen became general agent for the New York Association for Improving the Condition of the Poor (AICP), an organization dedicated to ameliorating the social milieu of impoverished people by pressuring the government to assume new obligations towards them. In 1894 the AICP had conceived the idea of vacation schools and recreation centers for tenement children and had successfully worked to have the city Board of Education assume responsibility for their administration three years later.[9] The organization also pressured the city to improve milk inspection so that poor communities could have an adequate milk supply.

Under Allen school affairs were a prime interest of the organization.[10] He set up a telephone hotline that principals could use if their pupils needed food or clothing. This endeavor led to a clash with New York City Superintendent of Schools, William Maxwell, who insisted that the education agency could handle student emergencies by itself. Allen responded with what would become a favorite theme of his; school record keeping was so inept that nobody knew which emergencies the education department could handle and which were beyond its capabilities. The controversy led the Board of Education to pass a resolution that principals should bring cases of want to the attention of charitable societies.[11]

Late in 1903 the city's Board of Estimate and Apportionment granted the school fund a 1904 appropriation of $16,300,000 which was $964,000 less than the Board of Education's request.[12] City comptroller Edward Grout accused the Board of Education of being extravagant and wasteful and argued that the schools could perform their operations on the appropriated sum if they started watching each dollar.[13] The board responded that it would have to cut programs beginning with a discontinuance of night schools, vacation schools, and recreation centers—all facilities used primarily by the poor—for a savings of approximately $75,000.

Allen joined other social workers at a meeting of the Civic Federation to condemn the board's action. They argued that the activities directed to the poor were not the weakest aspect of the school system and should not be eliminated.

The group appointed a committee with Allen as chair to investigate board records and propose alternative cuts. The committee wanted to compare school expenditures subject by subject, school by school to see the different results that various administrators achieved from given expenditures. It found the board's records so sparse and incomplete that it could not secure the information it needed. Allen asked Frederick Cleveland, a University of Pennsylvania classmate, then working as an accountant at Haskins and Sells, to review the records to see if the social workers had missed material of consequence; Cleveland read the papers and agreed they were inadequate to show where the board might save money.[14]

Allen's early fears about the affects of poor information at the education agency were fulfilled. The specific problem of losing evening and vacation schools was partially solved by the end of 1904; the board closed some recreation centers but agreed to continue all the evening sessions after receiving petitions from evening-school pupils and the Italian Educational Alliance.[15] But Allen and Cleveland decided the underlying problem remained; namely, the inadequacy of evidence about public endeavors. No improvements in public policy could take place until reformers had access to better information. The citizens needed an independent organization equipped to spur better data collection.[16]

In February 1905 Cleveland prepared a written prospectus for a permanent "Institute for Municipal Research" and gave it to Allen with the understanding that he would undertake to raise money for it.[17] The brief introduces a proposed organization that amalgamates taxpayer concerns over fraud and waste with social concerns for a better society. Under "Work to be Done" it lists scientific study of the framework of government, analysis of budgets and reports from the standpoint of results accomplished as well as sociological research on "the extent and cause of remediable conditions that indicate governmental responsibility for the physical deterioration of children . . . for preventable disease; for pauperism; for crime." It is clear from the prospectus that the Institute intended to act as a forum for pressuring government to become more active in social concerns (a stance similar to the AICP's). It is also clear that Allen and Cleveland were angry at the way the tenets of state laissez-faire resulted in horrendous living conditions for the poor. Theirs would not be an organization that would shrink from pointing a finger at governmental responsibility for bad conditions.

Allen shared the prospectus with R. Fulton Cutting, president of the AICP, and a major force in New York City's "good government" movement.[18] Late in 1905 Cutting indicated that he would support a year's trial of such an effort at $1,000/month to make an actual demonstration of what could be accomplished. He suggested that the Citizen's Union (of which he was president) should house what came to be called the Bureau of City Betterment and that Henry Bruere, who had been working under Allen at the AICP for a year, should serve as its director.[19]

Bruere plunged his small staff into several projects. They prepared a report on police efficiency which suggested that the department should study actual officer work loads and design job-related selection tests.[20] They cooperated with Mayor McClellan's Advisory Commission on Financial Administration and Accounting in its investigation of city reporting practices.

The success of the first half year's efforts led Cutting and Allen to approach John D. Rockefeller, Sr. and Andrew Carnegie to underwrite a permanent municipal-research institute and with their promise of financial support, the BMR was incorporated in May 1907.[21] At its inception the organization had a three-person chief executive of Allen, Bruere, and Cleveland, a trio who were soon dubbed "the ABC powers."[22] Two stories exist as to the origins of this unusual structural arrangement which violated the unity of command principle so popular among reformers at the time. In 1915 Cleveland recalled that Bruere was the original choice for director; Cleveland and Allen were added afterwards because of their expertise in accounting and fund raising, respectively.[23] Cutting, who had responsibility for the actual decision, recalled that he originally wanted Allen acting alone but that Allen requested a triumverate.[24] Whichever story reflects the actual progression of events, 1907–1908 Bureau publications list Allen as secretary, Bruere as director, and Cleveland as technical director; later materials list the three men alphabetically as directors.

The period when the triumverate worked together at the bureau was short. In September 1910 Cleveland took a temporary leave of absence to head President William Howard Taft's Commission on Economy and Efficiency affecting a hiatus in his bureau service. In January 1914 Bruere left the organization to serve as chamberlain in the reform administration of New York City Mayor John Purroy Mitchel leaving Allen and Cleveland as co-directors. Allen resigned in September 1914 and after this date efficient citizenship is no longer a central concept in the organization's work. Cleveland left in 1917.

While the triumverate was on board, the organization was led by three men who came from similar small-town backgrounds in the midwest. They had traveled east to attend Ivy League universities at the graduate level (the University of Pennsylvania for Allen and Cleveland, Harvard Law School for Bruere), moving from ethnically rather restricted environments to a very diverse big city. Each man was involved in or close to a profession (social work or accounting) that lay claim to bodies of knowledge and techniques which acolytes could learn from masters with experience. Unlike Cutting, part of whose prestige stemmed from his patrician upbringing, or Rockefeller and Carnegie, whose influence came from money, the ABC powers staked their bid for impact on what they could accomplish based on their educations and work-related backgrounds although neither Allen nor Bruere had a formal social-work degree.

Contemporaries agree that the men had different personalities. Allen is remembered as the most dynamic but also the most prickly. Robert Binkerd, Citizens Union secretary in 1908, said that at the BMR Allen was "the king pin, he was the driving force," but he was also "a tremendous egoist."[25] William Prendergast, New York City's reform comptroller from 1910–1917, recalled Allen as the zealot of the group, the one willing to use a meat axe to fight injustice, a style Prendergast admired.[26]

In addition, each man differentiated himself by writing about a different administrative function. Allen concentrated on schools and health. Much of the bureau's police work was drafted by Bruere. Cleveland's background made him the principal finance contact.

Of the three men only Cleveland had a professional background in his functional specialty. Allen had never served as a school administrator. Bruere had no police work experience. While this outsider stance may have facilitated their offering innovative solutions, it also brought charges of amateurism when the Bureau disagreed with operating bureaucrats. Although Massachusetts offered Allen the position of commissioner of industrial education in 1909[27], he also faced brickbats from political opponents who castigated him for not being an educational heavyweight with a degree in the subject from Harvard or Teachers College.[28] In such cases the bureau was faulted for not paying enough attention to a segmentation of expertise based on formal degrees. The BMR held that university certification was not the only way of gaining expertise; experience and on-the-job training could work equally well to qualify an individual as a problem solver.[29] Allen was acutely aware that his formal education had not provided him with all the information he needed to work with the poor.

The 1905 prospectus for the Institute of Municipal Research had noted that the new organization would have to be shielded in advance from the necessity of compromising its work or doing superficial projects to get financial support.[30] Because the BMR relied on private donations it had a virtual guarantee against governmental bodies stopping it or shifting its focus by threatening to withhold funds. But this guarantee only extended as long as it retained the confidence of major contributors.

Allen took most of the responsibility for fund raising. He met with donors and their lawyers and sometimes helped channel funds into particular projects. Between 1907 and 1914 Rockefeller emerged as the largest donor ($125,400) with his son, John Jr. and lawyer, Starr Murphy, often serving as intermediaries between him and the organization and providing positive feedback about the group's work.[31] He was followed by Cutting ($116,785) and Carnegie ($55,000).[32] The bureau could not afford to alienate any of these people.

The possibility of a rift can be gauged by comparing the tone of the original 1905 prospectus for the bureau put together by Cleveland and Allen and a 1907 pamphlet outlining the same theme but signed by the new BMR Board of Trustees. The two documents promise to do the same work but the tone of the latter is much more moderate. Gone is any mention that government policies may be responsible for the physical deterioration of children or pauperism. Instead the 1907 piece contains promises not to offend city officials.[33] The trustees are nowhere near as angry as the ABC powers at the state of urban life in turn-of-the-century America.

The Bureau and Scientific Management

The bureau announced that among its goals were to promote efficient and economical city government, promote scientific methods in reporting city business, secure constructive publicity for effective government projects and collect, classify, analyze, and publish municipal-agency facts.[34] To meet these objectives the organization intended to apply Taylor's shop management insights to city affairs.

Taylor's primary lesson for the organization was that performance issues are researchable; data collection is both feasible and useful as a basis for improving future actions. The organization certainly had little interest in Taylor's theories of wage incentives. The underlying rationale of shop management for it was that positive performance consequences emerged from research-based interventions, that knowledge gained through experiments could alter day-to-day production and services.

The BMR stressed the importance of establishing standards for city activities so worth could be measured against an ideal of maximum effectiveness rather than an average area's activity. The organization assumed experimentation would improve technical operations such as street cleaning or fingerprinting as well as helping the public resolve social questions such as the influence of stern versus humane prison regimes on recidivism.[35]

Taylor-style analysis of administrative strategies would yield comparative data that would allow a given city to gauge whether it should accept its own level of public health services, school promotion rates or utility charges. It would highlight the most effective techniques allowing people to "get done what all the time they had wanted to get done but didn't know how to do."[36]

Politicians and administrators varied in their response to the bureau's promotion of what it considered scientific study of government. Tammany Hall, locus of the Manhattan county Democratic machine, denounced the organization as alien to New York, citing the midwestern origins of its leaders.[37] One Manhattan official refused Bruere permission to see construction records that were legally available to the public; bureau staff had to physically inspect the streets to get the information they wanted.[38] School superintendent Maxwell refused permission to copy material from teacher records.[39]

An early opportunity for intervention came when the health department invited the bureau to help prepare an agency budget. The city legislature had pruned the department's past few requests leading the commissioner to believe that the agency would do better if it presented a budget that linked money to the activities on which it would be spent. To increase political accountability and a sense of the department's needs, the bureau suggested replacing an eleven-category budget with one that had thirty-four categories; a switch between categories would require legislative permission.[40]

Another key suggestion was holdings public hearing on the budget before it was approved so as to generate dialogue between citizens, administrators and legislators. As Cleveland explained

> Preliminary estimates and statements of departmental needs should be made public in order that the people . . . may discuss each of the issues presented . . . After full hearings as to relative needs, the board may with much intelligence fix the gross amounts to be appropriated.[41]

When comptroller Herman Metz saw the proposed budget at a Board of Estimate and Apportionment meeting, he invited the bureau to reorganize the finance department and improve its record keeping.[42] He stated that many private organizations had tried to help the city improve its budget making capabilities but only one—the BMR—contributed methods that were useful in practice.[43]

Shortly afterwards Police Commissioner Theodore Bingham asked the organization to help systematize the department's reporting function. The bureau lent him personnel to show departmental employees how to keep ledgers and prepare contracts. It urged the department not to waste uniformed officers in clerical jobs; the money saved could go toward the fight against crime.[44]

The bureau was responsible for many other studies that resulted in notable changes in New York's administrative practices including establishing new accounting methods, reorganizing the bureau of water revenue to increase collection of water rates by over $2 million a year, and opening a child hygiene section in the health department.[45] It became a "mecca and a model for governmental reform for the entire country."[46]

Beginning in 1909 the bureau performed work for other local governments and for nonprofit organizations. A report for the Pittsburgh public safety department, for example, stressed the need for better data collection to give the director adequate decision-making information (e.g., how do this year's number of complaints compare to last year's, do different detection methods result in increased arrests, etc.). It also urged job-related selection procedures for police rather than written exams and a training school for police and fire officers.[47]

The bureau shared the basic Progressive inclination to increase the scope of city and state action. In particular, it wanted city governments to assume social-service and health functions previously reserved for private philanthropy so that benefits that people had once gotten as charity could be received as rights.[48] It believed that citizens would only sanction this extension of government if agencies became more accountable and efficient.[49]

Although modern writers sometimes categorize the Bureau as an organization dedicated to economy, many of its proposals were certain to cost cities more money—at least in the short run. The bureau fought against reducing the allowance for New York's tenement department.[50] It successfully urged St. Paul, Minnesota to increase its health department appropriations so that the agency could hire a full-time administrator.[51] It championed placing free dental clinics in public schools.[52] A 1913 report urged upgrading first-year New York City patrolmen salaries from $800 to $1,000 per annum with the department rather than the individual officer paying all uniform and equipment costs.[53]

Textbooks and articles from its own era note that BMR proposals had the effect of raising municipal expenses.[54] Administrators for whom it consulted thanked it for setting the stage for the legislature's voting more liberal appropriations.[55]

Part of the confusion about the bureau's orientation stems from the fact that in promoting scientific management, BMR writers often used the term "efficiency" but gave it a somewhat different connotation than it has today. Contemporary writers tend to define efficiency in terms of most output/least input and the word often has definite bottom-cost implications. The bureau's circle preferred to define efficiency as doing those activities that the public wants done as well as possible at least expense, thus making explicit that efficient administration requires agency responsiveness to the public.[56] Cleveland notes that asking how we can make bureaucrats more efficient is synonymous with asking how we can make them more responsive.[57] He explains that

> The demand for efficiency must go farther than to . . . get a dollar for every dollar spent; it must constitute a demand that the government is doing the thing most needed, is conserving those ends and purposes which cannot be adequately reached through private undertakings.[58]

Bruere insists that New York's East River bridges might win efficiency medals from engineers but he finds them inefficient because they were designed without considering the needs of mass-transit users and so were not responsive to this population.[59] While a modern writer would most likely say these bridges were efficiently constructed but unresponsive to a segment of the community, Bruere simply labels them inefficient.

Because the bureau's notion of efficiency is tied to responsiveness, its suggestions often require greater expenditure of funds than an inefficient, unresponsive proposal would. Bruere says that efficiency translates into leading in supplying community welfare which for him means spending to promote health, education, and protection of citizens from landlords and employers.[60] At the time Bruere wrote, government was hardly involved in many of the activities he considered essential to efficiency and it was abundantly clear that the city would need additional revenues to enter these new spheres.

The bureau literature as a whole is much less concerned with saving money as a criterion for administrative success than are the contemporary reinventing government proposals. This difference occurs, at least in part, because the older literature takes a diametrically opposed standpoint on the relative task allocation for public and private sectors. The reinventing government literature wants to increase the private sector's role in social functions while the BMR insisted that further governmental action was necessary to ameliorate the lot of the poor. The BMR understood that money would be needed to finance increased government activity in the same way as the reinventing government authors trumpet that private endeavors will save taxpayer funds at least in the short run.

The National Performance Review insists that the central issue contemporary Americans face is not what government does but how it works.[61] One of the bureau's primary concerns, on the other hand, lay in abetting particular government actions (e.g., provision of medical services to the poor). Its interest in how government worked was instrumental; it saw structural and procedural changes as a means to prod the state to new programs in areas such as health and education. In regard to these programs the BMR prized value-for-money-spent rather than strict economy.

Educating Public Administrators

At a time when no American universities offered professional degrees in public administration, the bureau sought to make training available to public-sector managers. The first foray into this field occurred in the spring of 1907 when Allen, Bruere, and Cleveland gave a Public Business course at Columbia University.[62] The twenty-eight lectures opened by examining the similarities and differences between public and private administration. By having participants study legislative, executive, and electoral control of bureaucracies, this part of the course linked administration to politics.

The second section considered outside loci of influence on a given administrator's work including other agencies, nonprofit groups, and individual citizens. The teachers may have had their own struggles in mind when they included material on sharing records with outsiders. The concluding lectures focused on how public administrators could borrow business techniques such as centralizing staff functions.

A much more ambitious effort was started in 1911 when the bureau opened a training school with Harriman family money to prepare public-management specialists.[63] Students tended to be adult learners—many of whom already held degrees as doctors, lawyers, engineers, or accountants. The apprentice system formed the cornerstone of their education with each pupil assigned as an assistant to a staff member working on ongoing bureau projects. Remembering his own early intuition that book learning alone could not teach professionals how to respond in the field, Allen wanted students to "learn through doing, but not through doing alone, rather through doing plus observing freshly, critically, and optimistically."[64]

Additional time was spent at seminars where speakers included such scientific-management luminaries as Frederick Taylor, Harrington Emerson, L. Henry Gantt, and Frank and Lillian Gilbreth. Students also read books by Taylor and Emerson and by the bureau directors.[65]

Between 1911 and 1924, 1,468 people registered at the school, 1,299 part-time and 169 full-time. Of the latter group, 133 subsequently entered public service or taught public administration or finance. Twenty-five research bureau directors and nine city managers came from this contingent.[66] In 1913 the American Political Science Association appointed a committee to examine how universities could expand the bureau's work. This was professional acknowledgment that the organization had pioneered an effective way of offering practical training for the public sector.[67] Syracuse University was one of the first degree-granting institutions to borrow elements of the bureau's approach.

The BMR's role in bringing scientific management to public administration and in pioneering training for public managers was important in its time and is remembered briefly in contemporary discussions of the discipline's history. Those members of the public-administration community who have heard of the organization tend to think of it in terms of structural reorganizations and introduction of new accounting methods to city agencies, the type of work done for comptroller Metz or police commissioner Bingham, projects justified as an aid to managerial decision-making. Few people think of it as an organization dedicated to enlarging the role of citizens. Yet that is clearly the way the bureau envisioned itself and the way it was understood by its contemporaries both those who supported its position and those who prefered not to promote an active citizenry.

On the tenth anniversary of its founding, a supporter of the original bureau concept declared the organization "was premised on the proposition that it was an agency for the civic education of adults . . . the primary means of awakening citizens to a demand for improved public administration."[68] This facet of the bureau's work undergirds its citizen owner concept and extends the organization's work into explicitly political endeavors related to fostering citizens capable of exercising an active public role. The next two chapters examine this relatively neglected but conceptually crucial facet of the bureau's work. They reconstruct the organization's concept of citizen ownership of government and show the positions that this model led the bureau to take in a controversy over school politics. Once the ownership dimensions of efficient citizenship are understood their ramifications can be compared with those of the currently fashionable customer model.

CHAPTER 3

CITIZENS
AS OWNERS

In books and articles from 1906–1914, Allen, Bruere, and Cleveland stressed the importance of an active citizenry in spearheading administrative improvement. As a rationale for an enhanced public role, they hit on the metaphor of citizens as owner-shareholders of city corporations and argued that any enterprise needs the careful attention of the proprieter.[1]

In 1909 Cleveland urged New York's citizens to mind their own business—the public business. "In your city," he wrote, "is a great water-producing enterprise. You as citizens pay this water revenue. You, as citizens, have furnished this capital . . . This is *your* business. Are you *minding* your business?"[2] Owners with an expectation of improvement, owners willing to work for change, this was the only way to get more efficient city government.[3]

Cleveland contrasted the metropolis of his time and the eighteenth-century New England village. As he saw it, modern city denizens put the bulk of their energies into private matters such as careers and social life; traditional town folk cared about local government. Members of the community came together at town meetings to debate policy with reasonable intelligence; this historical experience showed that you could have a community that cared about government and took the time to learn about issues and debate them. You could have a community where citizens of average status and education behaved as if they owned the municipality.[4]

Modern governance would never improve unless citizens resumed their ownership obligations. This meant a commitment to

31

(1) instruct politicians and bureaucrats in community needs and remonstrate with them when they seemed to subvert public expectations, (2) enforce legal requirements that agencies keep records, and (3) protect conscientious public servants from false accusations. Getting involved was so crucial to municipal improvement that it became a duty. Democracy was seen as having no place for slackers; it demanded service. Citizens often complained about government service but if public tasks were not handled efficiently at least part of the problem was the citizen's own fault. Public administrators working alone would not be able to increase efficiency. Government could not improve without active citizens who assumed the interest and concern of enterprise owners.[5]

The bureau was optimistic enough to believe that this resumption of active citizenship was feasible. It assumed that civic pride, public spirit, and self-interest would propel citizens to accept ownership responsibilities as soon as they had information about what the city did and how scientific investigation of structures or procedures could increase concrete accomplishments. Information would produce a movement that would express citizen (rather than official) initiative for change. As Allen explained, "If there really was to be better government, the public must know how governing was done and must help those in power use better methods."[6]

The BMR bemoaned the fact that in its era most people got their city-performance information from personal observation, newspapers (which stressed scandals) and a few poorly written government reports.[7] With these sources few citizens knew if they were paying too much or too little for street paving. Few people understood if the city provided them with the best milk inspection procedures for lowering infant mortality. The way to get citizens to accept their ownership role was to make more information available to them in a form they could actually use. As Allen noted in a speech in Chicago

> There is one thing . . . about our major premise which is new in New York and that is the assumption that the great problem in municipal government is . . . to keep the public informed of what public officials are doing . . . So it is our very first and our exclusive motive, in the Bureau of Municipal Research, to bring about a method of talking about government and a method of govern-

ment that will keep you and me currently informed as to what our community needs.[8]

The BMR proposed to increase publicly-available information in four ways. First, it used common law and statutory rights to gain access to public records and make their data available in easy-to-comprehend form along with analysis on how procedural or structural change might enhance agency performance. Second, it prodded the city to keep clearer, more complete records. Third, it urged citizens to collect information on their own. Fourth, it promoted the need for frequent public hearings with interaction between citizens, administrators, and legislators.

A theme that runs through much bureau work is the city's obligation to prepare reports that are useful to a broad range of citizens. Cleveland argued that public-agency reports have two aims: they permit administrators to make decisions and they allow the public to follow the course of agency activities.[9] The documents available at the time obfuscated the issues; they could not be used to generate involvement in the public sphere. When the Municipal League of Los Angeles asked the BMR if the California city needed its own Bureau of Municipal Research, the answer was yes in part because Los Angeles did not provide its citizens with easy access to information.[10]

Cleveland and Allen criticized the fifth annual report of New York City's superintendent of schools for neglecting page headings and summary tables and for lack of boldface type to highlight key points; they wanted indexes, cross references, diagrams, and summaries.[11] Allen co-authored a book with a Teachers College professor which argued that the public would benefit from a uniform basis of reporting among school districts. Agencies should present information in a tempting way that made analysis and comparison possible; people needed facts "presented to disclose their significance."[12] The book showed people how to read the data that were available and make comparisons across jurisdictions on subjects such as which children were left back and which teaching techniques seemed to work with them.

Insiders who are responsible for operations rarely welcome the complaints of outsiders. Criticism of existing reports brought rejoinders from practicing administrators. Superintendent Maxwell complained to others in the educational community that leaflets to the general public were no place to criticize the school agency.[13] John Tildsley, a high school principal, defended the school report of 1905 on the ground that it was a mistake to let people know too much about educational problems and lose faith in the "responsible head of the great public school system."[14]

This comment led Allen to ask:

> What hope is there for democracy if its emblem, the public school, is not managed on democratic lines? If the public is to administer its own schools, it must be given current knowledge of results, including failures."[15]

At the heart of this debate is a difference in conception over the proper relationship between senior administrators (experts) and the public. Tildsley posits that an agency executive is owed respect and deference from a childlike citizenry whose members need to be shielded from bad news; the department has to restrict information to protect its functionary's aura of competence. Allen cannot abide the notion that citizens should lack information to protect the prestige of their own employees.

His assumption is that citizen-owners have the duty to take an active responsibility for improving government along with a perfect right to inquire into the affairs of their agents (the public administrators) at any time. Both Bruere and Allen suggest specific ways that citizens might exercise oversight. These ways center on citizen-initiated actions.

Bruere tells people how to test police efficiency. They should prepare a precinct map, list the regulations the police are supposed to enforce in the precinct and note patent violations. They should examine police records to see what the agency has done about such violations, record any arrests made and trace 200–500 cases through the courts. They should make unannounced visits to police posts to see what the officers are doing (as owners check on their workers) and analyze any complaints that other citizens have made to the precinct.[16]

Allen calls for volunteers to fill out scorecards comparing ventilation, play space, toilets, etc. in streets and schools in rich and poor neighborhoods. He urges his readers to make pin maps highlighting the neighborhoods that suffer from dirty streets or a higher-than-average incidence of death from contagious diseases. They should take these maps to the sanitation or health agencies and discuss the site of the pin clusters with administrators. People should ask their public employees what steps are being taken to minimize disparities in street cleaning and other government services. If the mapmakers conclude the agency would provide equal service if it had additional funds, they should attend the next budget hearing and express that sentiment. If they conclude the agency is unwilling to provide equal service, they should work to affect a change in personnel.[17]

A BMR bulletin suggests that readers use their vacation time to compare urban services (e.g., police courtesy, street clean-up) in New York and their destination city. When they return, they can let New York's administrators know about strategies that seem to work elsewhere.[18]

Both Allen and Bruere insist that schools must teach children to be efficient citizens. Rather than recommend additional study of American history which was the principal vehicle for inculcating citizenship at that time,[19] they praise education that revolves around urban problems with students encouraged to participate actively in their solution. The assumption is that acquiring active problem-solving skills is a prerequisite for a lifetime of efficient citizenship.

Allen commends a Brooklyn principal who asked students to report why they liked or disliked the school's introduction of the Gary plan, a change which involves a more intensive use of the school plant. The principal collected the information, gave the children feedback on what their classmates reported, and then asked them to suggest ways of making the innovation work, thus giving them practice in analyzing public-sector problems.[20] Bruere wants children to learn how to analyze agency reports and answer questions on health department efficiency based on infant mortality rates or the bacteria count in milk.[21]

The suggestion is made that pupils have to leave the classroom and go into the community to see the issues first hand. They get involved in housing by going to tenements, noting violations and reporting them to the authorities; they become interested in sanitation issues by reporting street cleaning violations.[22] With such training, people could enter into a life dedicated to municipal improvement.

One project the bureau used to kindle public interest in administration was the budget exhibit of 1908. Over 60,000 people visited an installation that used photographs, charts, and models to show how the city spent its $143,500,000 budget.[23] The exhibit aimed to show how public expenditures could give the citizens good value but how sometimes value-for-service was thwarted by fraud or waste. Visiters were to understand that "saving dollars could be used to save life, save health, or improve working conditions."[24]

A number of montages were designed to acquaint onlookers with services that the government provided them but of which they might have been unaware. One such installation displayed prototypes of contaminated food municipal inspectors had prevented merchants foisting on customers.

The most popular installation by far dealt with waste. Coat hooks which bureau staff had bought at a hardware store for six cents apiece proved the hit of the show when a sign nearby informed the public that the city had paid sixty cents a hook for identical merchandise![25] [The hook saga showed up several years later in an anti-Tammany campaign pamphlet which suggests that it was repeated over and over by opponents of the machine.[26]]

We know today that coat-hook-style installations are easy to crank out and subject to misinterpretation. Were the hooks really identical rather than similar? Was the city constrained to buy from certain suppliers even though others had less expensive merchandise? The organizers of the exhibit did not agonize over such questions because one of their purposes was to get publicity for the budget from an audience that did not normally concern itself with financial policy. They were willing to introduce a bit of vulgarity if the result was that truckers and longshoremen came to the hall and learned about various government services (as they did).[27] A city government textbook of that era praised the bureau for putting facts before the public "in the most accessible and striking form"[28] because this was the only way to interest a wide segment of the citizenry in working to improve municipal life. As we shall see later, however, this populist style was not appreciated by all bureau backers.

The Efficient Citizenship Mailings

The issue of style was raised most forcefully in connection with a series of miscellaneous publications the BMR produced and mailed to business, professional and labor organizations under the rubric *Efficient Citizenship* (1908–1913).[29] The first components of this series were postcards but soon the missives included pamphlets and circulars as well. In his memoirs Allen noted that he never sent the material in envelopes because he wanted the contents to entice readers.[30] In addition the bureau used brightly colored paper that was hard to misplace or confuse with other items but which seemed a garish touch to some readers.

A few examples give the flavor of the postcards. Publication No. 1 stressed that bureau work was practical and oriented towards bringing city agency techniques up-to-date. No. 45 reminded people that the commissioner of accounts was trying to pinpoint responsibility for defective fire hoses; citizens could bring information to him. No. 143 informed people that the Board of Education's finance committee had recently published a report. Under the title "Plenty of Time to Study the Budget," no. 163 noted when the Board of Estimate and Apportionment would hold public budget hearings, an innovation for which the bureau had fought. No. 495 showed an unclear table on infant mortality produced by a New York City agency and urged people to write the surgeon general in Washington to spearhead a drive for clear, comparative reports on health activities.

An early pamphlet (no. 180) discussed BMR recommendations to improve record keeping and investigation of complaints at New York City's Tenement House Department. Item no. 211 contained a 73 page topical index to the 1908 New York City schools report along with a list of other city school districts that provided an index with their annual reports to make the documents more useful to citizens. At least two pamphlets (nos. 386 and 416) compared non-promotion policies in different school districts based on a BMR survey of seventy-six communities. Number 515 reprinted a *School Review* article that argued high schools should enroll all children rather than only future leaders; the bureau asked readers for suggestions on how to increase the secondary-school population and promised to pass these ideas on to the education department. A constant theme is letting people know how they can get public-sector information and share their opinions with politicians and administrators. A 1913 pamphlet makes the reason for this information exchange clear: "The citizen shirks a large duty if he evades his part of the responsibility for efficient . . . work".[31]

Inclusiveness and Efficient Citizenship

One question that can be asked about efficient citizenship is how inclusive was the concept? Were women co-owners of their government? What role were the poor and members of ethnic minorities to play? If women and the poor were deliberately excluded as owners, the Bureau's work would be an odd model for modern times. It is not fair to ask turn-of-the-century writers to use a 1990s vocabulary on gender or class (e.g., to write "he or she" rather than "he") or to share our awareness of all the subtle barriers that preclude equal participation but it seems reasonable to demand a sensitivity to the basic contours of inclusion issues from those we look to for innovative ideas on citizenship.

The following two sub-sections examine the bureau's positions on gender and class separately. Gender was never a central issue on the bureau's agenda (and so we have much less evidence how bureau administrators treated women's issues in concrete instances) while the role of the poor is expansively articulated in bureau practice and thought. A difference exists between the bureau's attitude towards the gender variable which it predicted would have minimal substantive impact on politics and class which the administrators assumed would influence a citizen's relationship to issues. During the 1907–1914 period, New York City agencies debated a number of gender-related employment issues. The Board of Education, for example, debated whether male and female teachers should receive equal salaries until disparities in pay were removed by 1912. The school agency changed its original policy and began to permit women to continue their employment after they married. No evidence exists to indicate that the bureau was involved in these debates while it was an active force in articulating issues involving poverty and class and a key player in pressing for more government aid to the poor.

Gender

During the period when the bureau promoted the citizen-owner role, New York formally excluded women from the most elementary right of citizenship—the vote. The BMR saw this as a policy on its deathbed and supported the quick addition of females to the electorate although the administrators did not believe that this would affect substantive politics. They assumed women's views would parallel those of men in their social circumstances. Middle-class women would vote pretty much the same as middle-class men, and poorer women would show electoral patterns similar to those of poorer males. The bureau saw class rather than gender as the salient social component of political identity.[32]

In the meantime and afterwards the bureau expected women to participate in all the other duties of ownership. They were enjoined to make pin maps and bring them to administrators' attention; they were urged to attend budget hearings and make their views known. The Training School accepted women; the BMR employed females in professional positions. Although the bureau favored special restrictions on women's work hours (e.g., minimal night work), its general political position seems to have been that in theory at least women should be treated formally as men were treated and they would respond with attitudes and behaviors not too different from those of males. (Allen was way ahead of his time in believing that women could bear arms in the military![33]) Perhaps because of its generic theoretical position that gender would not affect substantive politics, the BMR never made women's equality a major theme in its publications.

Class

Allen argued that rich and poor were under the same obligation to serve as efficient citizens.[34] He urged everyone to get involved because the city needed all its people. He wanted the parents of poor children to monitor how New York's education system treated their children.

Rich and poor people were to get the same education for citizenship. In addition poor people needed socialization that would make them question the conditions they endured in the workplace;

they needed to develop the will to use the government to change problematic practices. The bureau saw altogether too much acquiescence to unconscionable employer-employee relations which could be changed with an education that stressed greater civic assertiveness. Within the confines of a capitalist system, Allen wanted to develop a more defiant and action-oriented worker class.[35]

The key to the bureau's class orientation is that the BMR believed efficiency had to be tested ultimately by the poor who were the ones who suffered most in its absence.[36] This drive towards inclusion was based on the assumption that "There is no relation between understanding public needs and possessing property" (an assumption that was very much at variance with the underlying framework of much of reform thought).[37]

The bureau never assumed poor citizens (many of whom were newly-arrived Catholic and Jewish immigrants) would approach public questions with the same mindset as middle-class WASPs. It saw each social and ethnic group as having its own needs and interests. For this reason it urged police departments in ethnically-diverse cities to hire Polish and Italian officers who would be responsive to their communities.[38] (The bureau leaders had to learn some of their tolerance by working in a diverse environment. When Allen once fired a man for making anti-semitic remarks, he admitted he would not have let the person go if the incident had occured right after he arrived from Lynn, Minnesota.)[39]

Active participation across the class and ethnicity spectrum was crucial because only a broad citizen initiative could set the stage for responsive, efficient government. No society was truly democratic if elections were the only time community interests affected politics[40]; the vote alone was insufficient to place citizens in control. Restricting nonelectoral activity to the rich meant perpetual inefficiency because public servants would be ignorant of the needs of the vast majority of owners. An issue such as unemployment, for example, could only be solved if the unemployed got involved with government officials and employers on committees to stimulate jobs.[41]

Yet the reality was that bureau activities attracted middle-class people. Allen acknowledged as much in one of his most dramatic indictments of injustice when he told his readers to ask themselves:

Am I doing things which would be considered crimes or misde-
meanors if done by residents of the slums? Am I indifferent to
wrongs committed by the government? Am I infinitely more
interested in surpressing flagrant vice than in preventing flagrant
injustice?[42]

Here Allen separated his readers from the slum dweller and urged
them to consider whether their acts would not be considered
crimes if committed by a poor person. The author admits that he is
talking to people who care about the poor rather than to the poor
themselves.

The breau tried to increase worker participation in politics. It
successfully campaigned to hold Bronx borough board meetings at
night to allow more people to come.[43] It included unions (as well as
business and professional groups) in its "Help-Your-City" campaign
where it asked organizations to collect suggestions on government
improvement and send them to the BMR.[44] One response was a
complaint that a private concession, Steeplechase Park and Huber's
Pavilion, had erected barriers preventing the public from access to
a beach at Coney Island. The BMR helped prepare the legal action
that dismantled the barriers and returned the beach to a broad
range of citizens.[45]

Allen considered it disastrous that Mayor Mitchel did not
appoint people who were broadly representative of New York's
entire electorate.[46] He echoed Theodore Roosevelt's famous comment, "Too much Fifth Avenue. Not enough First Avenue."

Yet the harsh economic demands on laborer time precluded
most blue-collar workers from becoming involved in the BMR's
drive for greater citizen concern. Bruere admitted that the organization had to show more examples of workers as efficient citizens to
make the concept truly inclusive but argued that ensuring such
class diversity was easier to propose than to actually effect.[47]

Then, as now, participation was easier for the rich. As wealthy
people can participate more fully in the social and economic lives of
their communities so too can they afford to spend more time fulfilling civic obligations. They are more likely to have control over
their work schedule. They can hire people to clean their dishes or
watch their children while they attend budget hearings. A 1989 survey found that people with family incomes over $50,000 were more

likely to participate in civic activities than those with incomes under $20,000; people who received means-tested benefits (e.g., AFDC, Medicaid, food stamps) were less likely to participate than the public at large.[48] We should expect such disparities to be even greater in 1906 or 1914 when blue-collar workers were more likely to work ten to twelve hours a day rather than eight. If most businesspeople and professionals lacked the hours or interest to immerse themselves in improving cities in a time-demanding way, it is easy to understand that comparatively few poor people became involved in bureau campaigns.

The bureau represented an organization staffed by middle-class professionals, dedicated to an agenda it believed was in the interests of the poor and financed by some of the most rapacious capitalists in America. The organization wanted to get the state involved in the fight against substandard housing and inadequate public health facilities. To wage battle, it relied on contributions from a man such as John Rockefeller, Sr. whose economic depradations played a role in making people poor in the first place.

That business leaders should support philanthropies pressuring the state to increase social-service funding was a prominent idea in the turn-of-the-century social work community from which Allen and Bruere hailed.[49] The bureau, however, went further than asking the rich to support state-financed programs. It urged the wealthy to underwrite a widespread citizen-owner voice in monitoring political and administrative actions. If different classes vary in their political needs (as the bureau believed), then the BMR was asking a man such as Rockefeller to pay up so that voices with a different message than his own could be heard. The untenable nature of this approach became clear in a controversy over school politics.

CHAPTER 4

CONTROVERSY OVER
THE SCHOOLS

In the spring of 1911 New York City's Board of Estimate and Apportionment appointed a three-person committee to secure a financial and educational study of the city's schools. Because it wanted additional facts made available to the public, the BMR was one of the prime supporters of this endeavor. Bruere drafted the resolution introduced at the Board of Estimate meeting authorizing the inquiry.[1]

The committee—Chairman John Purroy Mitchel (then president of the city's Board of Aldermen), Cyrus Miller (Bronx borough president), and William Prendergast (city comptroller)—hired Paul Hanus, a professor of education at Harvard University, to oversee the educational portion of the study. Research was to take place from June 1 to December 31, 1911. The Board of Estimate agreed that it might make available additional time to prepare the documents until July 1, 1912.[2] Part of Hanus' task was to nominate eleven specialists to execute reports on different facets of the educational system with the committee having the right to reject any of the candidates.

Political hot potatoes confronted anyone proposing to analyze New York's schools. In 1911, Progressive educational administrators favored a school-governance model that tended to limit popular participation in decision-making in three ways.[3] First, state legislatures separated school governance from city politics which was seen as corrupt and tainted. The mayor and other elected municipal officials retained control over fire, police, and sanitation functions but control of public schooling was placed under the authority of a separately elected Board of Education. This board was generally elected in a nonpartisan, at-large contest where participation was smaller than in the municipal elections and more skewed to the Anglo-Saxon Protestant middle class, thus eliminating a large immigrant presence.

Second, boards of education were made smaller and less representative of all the diverse groups in the city. At-large elections in particular made it difficult for minority ethnic and religious communities to elect their own representatives. Third, boards were expected to delegate extensively to appointed superintendents who made decisions based on professional norms (i.e., expertise) rather than on community needs as articulated through the political process.

Charles Eliot, president of Harvard University, was a supporter of this model. He argued that the state had a right to direct the city's educational structure because if urban problems were allowed to grow, they would eventually engulf the whole state. He believed that large boards attracted mediocre people, i.e., those who had never succeeded in business and owned little property. Accordingly, he favored a board of seven people. He wanted all boards to have a limited role as their members were amateurs and only experts knew how to perform complex tasks.[4]

This scenario was at odds with New York's actual situation where the mayor appointed the board of education, the municipal government retained considerable fiscal authority over the schools (the Board of Estimate appropriated school fund money) and the large, forty-six person board of education took a more active decision-making role than the educational administration community preferred. The stage was set for conflict between educational administrators surveying the schools and New York City's politicians—a kind of conflict where the modern literature argues professionalization worked against popular participation, particularly among Catholic immigrant groups, and control by officials elected from a constituency including working-class voters.[5]

Hanus nominated Professor Ernest Moore from Yale University to report on the board of education telling him

> What I am particularly anxious to ascertain is whether the conception of its functions which the board of education has is well

defined; whether that conception is justified and whether the organization and methods of the board tend toward efficiency.[6]

Moore was a wholehearted follower of the educational administration model. Because he believed "the worst misfortune that can happen to a school system is to fall into the hands of the City Hall," he saw his mission as rescuing New York's children from being "exposed to the taint of current municipal politics."[7] He advocated a small board that would delegate extensively to the superintendent.

During the summer of 1911 Allen met with Hanus several times to discuss the survey but the atmosphere quickly soured as the two men realized their goals were diametrically opposed.[8] Allen favored a model that encouraged popular participation and monitoring in line with the citizen-owner concept. He preferred a system controlled by elected city officials and a large, representative board of education. Since he did not believe property ownership necessarily qualified a person to pursue public affairs, he differed with Eliot or Hanus over the utility of smaller, less representative boards. As a matter of fact the bureau believed that New York City's board was too quick to abdicate to departmental experts the key function of molding policy.[9]

The bureau had long been against state-created boards to oversee municipal transportation or utilities. Citizens could not act like owners if control over vital functions was deliberately taken out of their hands and without a citizen-owner presence efficiency in these functions would suffer.[10] For the same reason the BMR also preferred city control over schools. Hanus supported Moore.

Interestingly, Hanus, Moore, and Allen all referred to scientific management to justify their positions. The educational administrators argued that Taylor's theory required experts to make decisions.[11] The bureau believed that scientific management privileged information itself above hierarchical standing or generic educational background. Once lay people had information about a particular controversy they could be as useful as degree-certified experts in decision-making. With this interpretation, scientific management does not preclude lay participation in decisions but rather it fosters greater dissemination of information which, in turn, increases the viability of popular involvement.

As the draft reports appeared, Mitchel's committee expressed unhappiness about Moore's work and a disinclination to accept it. Although Mitchel did favor reducing the board's size, he was committed to strong city government with elected municipal officials controlling schools as they did other local activities, a stance at odds with any insistence on professional control.[12]

In the summer of 1912 the committee sent letters to several specialists (including Moore) asking questions (some of them rather hostile) about the work. Hanus objected to this direct contact with the specialists as interference with his function.[13] When the committee persisted in requiring answers to its queries, Moore responded in words that clearly show his disdain for mere politicians questioning experts such as himself. In one letter he wrote, "My report was not intended to verify your opinions . . . it was intended to teach you and your colleagues something about the proper way to administer a school system."[14] In another he continued

> Your conception of the proper way to run a school system and my experience . . . are at such variance that it would be futile to even attempt to convert you from your opinions. I do not feel any obligation to attempt so foolish a task."[15]

Hanus and Moore realized they would need powerful allies if they were to challenge Mitchel in the public arena. They approached Jerome Greene—manager of the Rockefeller Institute for Medical Research and member of the Rockefeller-controlled General Education Board—to try to salvage Moore's report.[16] Greene favored small boards that delegated extensively to their superintendents; he believed that members of New York's Board of Education were basically unintelligent mediocrities.[17]

The correspondence between the three men shows clearly that Hanus and Moore considered the bureau—particularly in the person of William Allen—to be the major player on the side of an active Board of Education. They believed that the bureau, to promote a more active (to them interfering) citizenry, was stirring up Mitchel to reject Moore's advice. Much of the anger of these two educational administrators was directed against Allen's "pernicious and unwarranted meddling"[18] which they believed had caused the committee to take such a strong stand on the issue of political control.

Greene agreed that the imbroglio emanated from "the machinations of Allen."[19] Mitchel was simply under the thumb of bureau people with undesirable ideas.[20] Supporters of good government had to find a way to stop the BMR from urging lay people to take a larger role in school and police affairs.[21]

In October 1912 the Board of Estimate and Apportionment published an eleven-volume Hanus report. It refused to accept Moore's contribution, calling it "[A] false, inaccurate and misleading document."[22] Frank Goodnow and Frederick Howe were hired to write another report on the Board of Education.[23] (Perhaps because these scholars came from political science rather than educational administration, they concluded that the Board of Education should not be separated from control by city officials.)

During this period the bureau used its efficient citizenship mailings to support the Board of Estimate's stand on the need for an active board of education that would be tied to city government. In November 1912 the BMR mailed a postcard asserting that no facts supported Moore's contention that an active Board of Education prevents professional staff from doing their jobs.[24]

In 1913, the bureau reprinted Thomas Churchill's acceptance speech on becoming president of New York's Board of Education. Churchill succinctly confronted the politics-expertise dichotomy by arguing that the board could not delegate to professionals basic curriculum-development responsibility. The board was supposed to find out what type of curriculum people wanted and this concern for citizen desires was at the core of good, public education. Churchill gave short shrift to the claims of expertise for essential control, noting that "[T]he history of education reeks with failures springing from the imposition of systems devised by experts."[25]

The role of the bureau in the school controversy left Hanus and Moore with a sense of outrage. Moore briefly contemplated suing the BMR for libel because a November 1912 efficient citizenship postcard intimated that he had done a poor job of supporting his demand for expert control.[26] Hanus shared his discomfiture with Charles W. Eliot, Harvard's president, and a prominent supporter of a strong superintendent model. Eliot expressed surprise that the Rockefeller interests funded a man who had Allen's unacceptable political views and argued that withholding Rockefeller money could be used as a lever to force Allen from his position; this would be a good thing because the man "does not seem to be a creditable agent for a body of respectable citizens trying to do good."[27]

Greene shared with Moore the notion that Allen's strength lay in the support of rich men.[28] In mulling over BMR policy, Greene had already acknowledged to himself that Rockefeller money might constitute a trump card in forcing the organization to abandon the quest for more citizen involvement. A private memorandum that he wrote to himself notes that "the Bureau of Municipal Research is not likely to do anything to permanently alienate our support."[29] In a letter to Hanus he adds that Allen's

> conception of the bureau's function as a publicity agent . . . rather than as a calm, dispassionate, detached instrument for scientific investigation and report, is a very vital matter which should, I think, be brought immediately to the attention of the backers of the bureau.[30]

John D. Rockefeller, Sr. was the bureau's single largest donor. The first documented indication of concern from this quarter appears in a November 1912 letter from his lawyer, Starr Murphy, to Allen voicing two complaints: (1) the bureau generated too much controversy over educational politics and (2) the efficient citizenship postcards engaged in contentious publicity in areas that were better left to professional decision-makers.[31] Rockefeller objected both to the organization's substantive stand on educational politics and to its involving the public in school issues.

The efficient citizenship mailings soon emerged as a major bone of contention between the antagonists. As noted earlier, the bureau deliberately sent its messages to a wide range of organizations including trade unions and printed them in a manner designed to attract immediate perusal, e.g., by using brightly colored paper stock. For Hanus this strategy revealed a penchant for "publicity hysteria."[32] Greene labeled the series "rubbish" and a "laughing stock."[33]

In a letter to Allen, Greene defined in somewhat more moderate language their differences over how to run a bureau of municipal research:

It seems to me that in the long run the influence of such a bureau is enormously enhanced if it confines its function to investigation, study and recommendation . . . You evidently . . . consider that the Bureau has an additional function, namely that of promotion, persuasion and agitation . . . My own opinion, however, is that if the Bureau abstains entirely from the promotion, persuasion and agitation side of its work, its power for good would, in the long run, be increased.[34]

Early in May 1913 John Rockefeller, Jr. asked Bruere in conversation why so many of the efficient citizenship pieces dealt with school issues. Allen replied in a letter that the organization had special appropriations for this subject.[35] (No evidence exists today that the bureau had special appropriations for school issues as a whole. The Bureau had received gifts to do mailings on school children health and on an educational conference held in St. Louis.

On May 9, 1913, Rockefeller, Jr. asked Abraham Flexner, assistant secretary of the General Education Board (GEB), to familiarize himself with the bureau's methods of doing educational research.[36] Flexner had joined the GEB in 1913 after completing a famous critique of medical education sponsored by the Carnegie Foundation for the Advancement of Teaching and was considered an educational improvement expert.[37]

Rockefeller's request must have galled Allen who considered Flexner critical of earlier work the bureau had done in Wisconsin[38] but no hint of any discomfiture slips when he writes to John Jr. apologizing if the efficient citizenship series lacked dignity and suggesting that the bureau could prepare better pamphlets if it had more money.[39] At this point he treads warily; he wants to keep Rockefeller's patronage but is not prepared to change his political opinions or methods to placate a donor.

The apology was insufficient to divert the impending investigation. In the fall of 1913 the bureau agreed that the General Education Board would fund a study by Flexner on the BMR's educational work.[40] Allen noted that a charged atmosphere existed at the time with the bureau being faulted for trying to help "Catholicism," an imputation that stems from the BMR's educational preferences giving more potential power to the heavily Catholic immigrant groups.[41]

Aspects of the study suggest that Flexner had a particular conclusion in mind right from the start. He used Hanus as a consultant even though it was widely known in the educational community that the Harvard professor loathed Allen.[42] Flexner's assistant, Frank Bachman, had previously worked with Hanus in the New York school survey, a fact that is not mentioned in the Flexner document.[43] Also unmentioned are all positive comments on the bureau that Flexner received from school superintendents and principals who had worked with Allen over the years.[44] One of these superintendents seems to have totally mistaken what the Rockefellers might want and lauded the BMR for awakening interest in politics among the general public![45]

Flexner's report downgrades the importance of the bureau's educational work. In particular, it castigates the bureau's attempts at involving the public instead of letting professionals make decisions. Most of the obloquy falls on the efficient citizenship pieces which were labelled "trivial and even vulgar . . . designed to arrest attention by their explosive character . . . their high coloring frequently suggests partisanship and controversy."[46]

Flexner belittles the bureau's invitation to citizens to compare school conditions in rich and poor neighborhoods, arguing that everyone knew that some plants were in better shape than others. He criticizes the bureau's campaign for outside cooperation with schools, asserting instead that educational institutions should move with caution in inviting participation of outsiders. He also mentions the political situation—the bureau was associated with a faction that wanted the Board of Education to have more control over the city's schools.

Once the report was available, Starr Murphy told Rockefeller, Jr. that the bureau's educational and health work did more harm than good and that the solution was to push the bureau's trustees to confine its mission to reorganizing city agencies on a sound financial basis.[47] Henry Pritchett of the Carnegie Foundation agreed that the organization was too intent on involving the public in a revivalist manner.[48] Murphy assumed the problem would be getting R. Fulton Cutting, the trustees' president, to accede to a change.

At first, Cutting supported the bureau. On school politics his sympathies were akin to Allen's. In 1905, he had collaborated with Allen and Cleveland in an appeal to the Board of Education to generate more performance data to hold professional staff accountable for following board policies. He wanted the board to have sufficient information to act independently in the policy-making arena.[49]

Cutting argued that Flexner's unease with the BMR simply reflected the different agendas of academic and practical people. The bureau was founded to present scientific management research in such a way that the public could use it for political action. Publicity was inherent in its mission. Its publications were intended to interest a mass audience rather than the few.[50]

But the organization could not ignore the threat of Rockefeller Sr. withdrawing financial support. Allen asserted that at this point Rockefeller offered the bureau $10,000 over a five-year period if the organization would get out of the school field, stop its publicity work, and confine its research to New York City.[51] Cleveland argued that no such explicit quid pro quo dominated the discussions.[52] But a letter from Cutting to Greene shows the crucial bureau trustee believed that Rockefeller would give $2,000/year to the BMR only on condition that it remained silent on educational issues and made other changes.[53]

On February 28, 1914 Allen and Cleveland had a six-hour meeting to discuss the BMR's future.[54] (Bruere had left in January to serve as city chamberlain.) Allen argued that the bureau should continue on its original path. Even if this meant losing Rockefeller support, promoting an active citizenry had to remain the focus of bureau policy. Cleveland urged taking a more cautious approach to mass publicity.

An explanation is needed for Cleveland's willingness to change orientation even though up to that time his own writings at the bureau had favored the efficient citizenship concept. One possibility is that his ideas had actually changed over time and that by 1914 he no longer considered a citizen-owner model indispensable for reform. In her work on the history of budgeting, Irene Rubin notes that Cleveland was less intent on holding public budget hearings after his experience with President Taft's efficiency commission than he had been previously. She attributes this change to his exposure to the more conservative atmosphere of the federal administration in Washington.[55]

While the commission experience may have influenced his political persona, it cannot be considered a watershed event that alienated him from all intent to promote an active citizenry; his 1913 book, *Organized Democracy*, published after he completed his commission work, continues to promote efficient citizenship. A counterexplanation may be that he had always had a more malleable personality in his relations with authority and that is why he (rather than Allen) was chosen to chair the 1912 Taft commission even though both men were interviewed for the position.

Whatever the psychological reasons, the two men who had once agreed on so much about politics could now not reach a compromise. Cleveland resigned on March 2. The trustees refused to accept the resignation; instead, they gave Allen a leave to do research at the University of Wisconsin and put Cleveland in complete control of the bureau in his absence.[56]

The *New York Times* sided with Cleveland and the trustees in this dispute. The newspaper argued that the bureau should distribute less publicity about contentious ongoing problems. It upheld Rockefeller's right to withhold his money from organizations with whose policies he disagreed.[57]

On April 10, Cutting and another BMR trustee met with John Jr. to discuss his family's contributions; when Rockefeller raised the question of whether the bureau would continue to advocate mass publicity, he was told to speak to a BMR director. The next day he met with Cleveland who told him a new direction would prevail.[58] After that meeting, John Jr. wrote to a General Electric executive that the bureau was reorganizing and would distribute no more "undignified" efficient citizenship pamphlets.[59]

In September 1914 Allen resigned under pressure that a vote to oust him would pass at the trustees meeting in November.[60] Cutting then wrote to Greene asking for $2,000 as Rockefeller's conditions had been met.[61]

During Cleveland's 1914–1917 tenure as sole director, the bureau was a more restrained organization than it had been in its earliest years. Cleveland sent drafts of his material to Flexner and Greene for their views before publication; he promised Greene to limit circulation on papers dealing with the budget.[62] Cutting pleaded with Starr Murphy to allow the organization to go to the public as a last resort if the bureaucracy would not enact reforms but the lawyer replied that the BMR had to learn to stay away from propaganda.[63] At a meeting of the National Municipal League a Wisconsin reformer noted the change of direction:

> Ten years ago to-morrow there was established in New York City the bureau of municipal research . . . Now that movement is shipwrecked and has become largely a private agreement between the board of trustees of the bureau and the city officials . . . without even letting the public know what was being done.[64]

With some justice Allen accused Rockefeller of chloroforming the municipal efficiency movement.[65]

During this period Allen and Cleveland had a revealing debate over revisions to the Maryland constitution which Cleveland had helped to enact.[66] Cleveland expressed satisfaction with constitutional provisions that allowed the governor to give reasons for specific appropriation requests; Allen wanted the governor mandated to make such explanations so that the public would be certain to have this information. Cleveland accepted a system that failed to require public hearings before a budget came up in the legislature; Allen insisted on such hearings. Cleveland headed a major organization that was well funded by leading philanthropists but that had strayed from its original mission as defined by the man himself. Allen remained true to his early vision.

After the Fall

In 1915, Allen founded the Institute of Public Service, another organization dedicated to improving the performance of city agencies. From this platform he intended to continue the campaign for efficient citizenship through a series of pamphlets and postcards captioned *Public Service*.[67]

Unfortunately, Allen never lost his sense of the wrong that he believed had been done him by the Rockefeller interests. For years he attacked the family in shrill *Public Service* postcards that were crammed with type and barely understandable. During the same period he wrote innumerable letters to John Jr. asking him to reconsider his decision on efficient citizenship.[68] It is a sad summation to a distinguished career that on one of his 1925 letters a Rockefeller

counsel appended the handwritten note "Allen is a crank," and that by
that time on the subject of the Rockefellers the complaint was true.[69]

Allen noted in his memoirs that money could have a corrosive
impact on administrative research and efforts at political reform.[70]
Both government agencies and private philanthropists have vested
interests and consciously or subconsciously they may try to protect
these interests through their funding allocations. Researchers
often have to take into account the mindset of their backers in
deciding on projects and dissemination strategies. Reformers have
to tread warily in choosing abuses to confront.

The BMR considered citizens to be the owners of city government including the school agency and directed their message to
these shareholders. They did not reflect on how their message
would play among their own financial backers. This naivete left the
organization relatively defenseless against an onslaught fuelled by
people associated with its premier donor. The BMR's 1914 reorganization effectively buried the efficient citizenship concept in public-administration discourse so that a strong, vibrant citizen-owner
model tuned to modern vocabulary is not available to confront the
customer model offered by Osborne and Gaebler and the National
Performance Review. Inquiry itself has suffered from the role
money played in the progression of the field's ideas.

Using what we know of the bureau model, however, it is possible to see how a citizen-owner approach would differ in its political
implications from the customer construct. The next chapter
explains what reconstructing an ownership model means for the
direction of modern administrative reform in terms of increasing
the emphasis on citizen action rather than concentrating solely on
managerial change. The question of whether such reconstruction is
a realistic option is also considered.

CHAPTER 5

ANALYSIS

The relevance of the historical case study presented in the last three chapters stems from the Bureau's wholistic stance on the changes the nation must undertake to significantly improve public-sector performance. Both proponents of reinventing government and efficient citizenship want to change public organizations. Their models use different strategies because the contemporary model views the public as customers who react to what a company offers while the older construct gives the public a proactive role.

Historians say an era is known by the metaphors it keeps.[1] Both the old and the new reformers borrowed their analogies from the business world. If the metaphors people use are an index to their values, than this practice suggests that they assumed the notion of private-enterprise efficiency had positive connotations for their audiences. The people they wanted to reach considered the customer or owner roles as ones that gave a certain satisfaction. In a society with different values, reformers would borrow metaphors from the military or the church.

Business terms probably did create a positive aura for both sets of reformers but a downside of this strategy is that the ensuing models are vulnerable to the charge of glossing over important differences between the private sector and government. The danger is that when one entity (government) is translated into another (business), important features of the phenomenon under translation can get lost. Public agencies are not simply a set of firms that provide marketlike services; to speak of them solely in market terms is to reduce their unique essence.

From a philosophical viewpoint we cannot neatly encapsulate government-citizen relations in either the ownership or customer metaphor. Each attempt betrays logical inconsistencies which are best apprehended through examining the flaws in correspondence inherent in each analogy.

Owners and Customers

Owners

Legal rights of possession distinguish business owners who have unique economic rights in the enterprise and the authority to direct its course. The most fundamental difference between business and citizen ownership relates to economic rights. When ownership is used as a political metaphor, no heed is paid to its pecuniary implications. The bureau writers understood that people do not buy American citizenship or sell it at a profit. The metaphor is clearly intended to relate only to the aspect of ultimate control. The constitution says that we the people established the central legal document ordaining the government; we the people should have a concern for directing the course of this enterprise.

But an assumption that private-sector ownership translates into control founders on the difficulties real-world owners have directing their businesses. The owners who invest maximum energy in and make ultimate decisions for enterprises tend to be sole proprieters. Most corporate shareholders have little interest in controlling the companies in which they invest money; they have inadequate time, information, and expertise to get involved in decision making. These shareholders are better models of passivity than of active control agents.

As early as 1927 a public-administration textbook asserted that citizen owners have more in common with corporate shareholders than with sole proprieters.[2] Both citizens and shareholders form large, variegated bodies of people who are often ignorant of the identity of their fellow owners and find it difficult to coordinate any attempt at control. Because the mass of shareholders and citizens lack time, information, and interest to direct the enterprise over which they have ultimate rights in theory, the ownership metaphor may actually be more useful at explaining why few citizens get involved than in giving them a rationale to do so.

Customers

The customer metaphor is equally flawed. In the private market customers choose among products and services. While they may not like the range of items businesses offer, they tend to enter transactions voluntarily and prefer getting the car or haircut they purchase to having no car or haircut at all.

Many public agency clients would prefer to have no contact with the bureaucracy. This category of involuntary customer contains the owners and managers of many regulated enterprises. It includes most criminal-justice clients (e.g., defendants at trial, prisoners, people on probation or parole). It even includes some people getting economic benefits from the government such as individuals on social security who would have preferred to invest their retirement funds on their own. Should we use the term customer to refer to people who do not want the services legislation ordains for them? Some Internal Revenue Service employees receiving Total Quality Management training thought not; they protested that the word customer was inappropriate for describing American taxpayers![3]

By choosing a market niche businesses define their customer targets; the firm that targets luxury car buyers deploys different production and marketing strategies than the one whose customers want to pay $15,000 for an automobile.[4] Delighting customers is relatively easy when the clients represent a well-defined group whose members have similar requirements in terms of the product they are purchasing.

Public agencies, on the other hand, have many potential customer groups including

> those who immediately present themselves for the service, those who may be waiting for the service, those who may need the service even though they are not actively seeking it, future generations of service recipients and friends of the immediate recipient.[5]

Strong conflicts of interest exist among people interacting with any given bureau making it difficult for many departments to identify who their customers are and how they can satisfy customer needs. If food inspection is a bureau's function, who is the agency's customer—Tina, a restaurant owner or Tom, a consumer of restaurant meals? Tom and Tina may have different definitions of responsive service.

Who is the customer of a school department? The students? the parents? all the adults in the community? Assume a locale where a majority of students are satisfied with a given school environment. The voters send the incumbent Board of Education packing and initiate a radically different environment. Is this a victory for customers or not? Lack of agreement should alert us to conceptual weaknesses in appropriating the term.

This problem is particularly evident for organizations with stewardship obligations.[6] The Environmental Protection Agency and the Forest Service are supposed to serve one set of clients today while protecting another in the future. The more assiduously these organizations cultivate today's customers, the less rigorous may be their performance of their stewardship duties. It may well be impossible to follow the precept of Total Quality Management and delight both sets of clients.

The weakest attribute of the customer model seems to be its assumption that satisfaction with government will increase if agencies treat citizens as business treats customers. The National Performance Review states explicitly that its goal is to equal the best in business, to give its customers "the level of quality Americans enjoy every day in the private marketplace."[7] This aim only makes sense if a significant gap currently exists in the quality of service people receive in the two sectors. Those people responsible for the National Performance Review obviously believe such a gap exists. Their reports constantly denigrate all past government service efforts in favor of the treatment accorded customers by firms such as Walt Disney. James King, the director of the federal Office of Personnel Management, likes to call his bureau "OPM Inc." to show that he sees corporations as the model for effective customer service.[8] But hard evidence (as opposed to an anecdote here, an anecdote there) for different service standards is scarce. The Gore report says that customer-service improvement is necessary to raise public faith in the government. Yet national opinion surveys generally show that citizens perceive their encounters with public bureaucracies in a favorable light.[9] A recent survey of Georgia residents' attitudes towards public (e.g., post offices, fire protection, health clinics) and private (e.g., banks, private mail carriers) service providers found no systematic ratings differences by sector.[10] If public service is inherently inferior to that offered by private firms, this distinciton does not seem to shape citizen attitudes.

In lauding the service customers receive from businesses the reinventing government proposals may be promoting a phanthom. Many private-sector organizations are seen by their clients as bureaucracies awash in red tape with little interest in the concerns of the average customer.

In the same way that the ownership model scants differences between the control exercised by sole proprieters and corporate shareholders, the customer scenario neglects variations in the treatment clients receive from large and small businesses. The corner grocer may be extremely responsive to the needs of each customer. Health insurers and banks are likely to have bureaucratic structures with many rules and procedures that clients characterize as red tape; street-level workers at these private firms cannot make exceptions to suit a unique contingency.

The same people who complain about the long line at the motor vehicle bureau are likely to inveigh against the horrendous wait for a teller or a claims agent. The man or woman who hates redundant forms that do not make sense at the tax office is likely to find equally overbearing forms tendered by an insurance agent. Geting your account cleared after a department-store computer has double billed you for shampoo is as frustrating as trying to get a social-services agency to recalculate your benefit after its computer has also made a mistake.

Whenever an organization grows large and geographically dispersed, the top maintains control through written rules and forms that limit the discretion of street-level employees. If public agencies adopted the interaction strategies large businesses actually use with the bulk of their individual clients, efficient, responsive service would not necessarily be the norm. Changing citizens into customers is not a useful solution to government's problems because actual private-sector customers encounter service inadequacies of their own.

One of the ironies of the NPR is that by eliminating politics and substantive policymaking the document trivializes what makes for effective service in public or private enterprises—even its discussion of customer relations is flawed. The report assumes that customers care quite a bit about speed and courtesy, almost nothing about the products or services that are offered to them. But this assumption hardly squares with private-sector reality. People are more likely to choose a bank for its home improvement loan or CD rates than for the size of its teller lines. Social security beneficiaries—even in the limited role of customers—might prefer to see an improvement in product lines (e.g., giving a spouse income credit for housework) over an improvement in how quickly the staff returns telephone calls. But the NPR limits its discussion to making faster and safer payments—a small part of the customer-service role.

The analysis shows that neither metaphor captures all the complexity of the public-agency relationship. While this inability means that we have to be cautious in attributing characteristics to the objects compared based on expectations raised by the verbal devices themselves, it does not imply that we dare disregard either metaphor's implications for political debate. The ultimate worth of a political metaphor does not depend on its accuracy but rather on the insights it provides in interpreting social phenomena. The fate of the owner and customer analogies should depend on the importance of the particular aspects of the government-public relationship that each highlights. The argument of this book is that each metaphor organizes and filters our perception of the citizen-agency relationship in quite different ways. These permutations lead inexorably to variant change prescriptions to improve government. Before deciding the place to give each analogy in our vocabulary we must analyze the path to change that each fosters. The owner and customer metaphors differ in their implications for citizen action and sense of community. Each of these crucial differences can be examined in turn.

Consequences of the Metaphors

Action

Reinventing government centers on how public administrators can satisfy customers. Administrators are the actors; they survey client attitudes, make services convenient, empower their

subordinates, decide which programs to contract out or decentral-
ize—in many ways acting as owners do in private business.
Osborne and Gaebler's list of necessary changes to improve confidence in government include: steering rather than rowing, empowering rather than serving, injecting competition into service
delivery, having organizations that are mission rather than rule
driven, results-oriented government, customer-driven government,
enterprising government, government that prevents rather than
cures and decentralized government.[11]

All these reforms entail change in administrative work routines, bureaucratic cultures and agency procedures to allow various
departments to develop entrepeneurs and leaders. Since members
of the public are only the recipients of administrative action, little
thought is directed to changing their routines to increase the prob-
ability that leaders will emerge from their ranks. The assumption is
that changing bureaucratic structures and relationships will yield a
more sensitive and responsive public service.

The customer metaphor is inappropriate for conferring an
active, agenda-setting role. When government officials want private
elites to help set the agenda for agencies the owner metaphor is
naturally used even in modern times because owners set an enterprise's course. Ronald Reagan, in inaugurating the President's Private Sector Survey on Cost Control (informally known as the Grace
Commission) in 1982, asked business leaders to suggest change
strategies and told them to approach their analysis as if they were
planning to own the agencies.[12] He did not ask them to assume they
were customers because customers do not write change plans or
otherwise direct the course of private sector firms.

Efficient citizenship extends this metaphor from elites to a
wider audience. It assumes citizens act. They monitor agencies and
make their preferences known. Reform requires public empower-
ment through citizenship education and constant information
exchange. Although structural change may also be necessary, the
assumption is that government will not work without citizen
involvement. Bruere argued that a city should worry first about getting information to the public. After this is done people can debate
structural change through citizen rather than official initiative.[13]

The bureau literature is directed by and large at lay audiences.
It tells lay people why they must act and which channels are avail-

able to them. Cleveland reminds his readers that new administrators often want to make improvements; to prevent these public employees from getting caught up in the status quo citizens must interact with them and press for greater efficiency.[14] In this scenario the professional needs the support of an informed conscientious public to get the job done correctly. The protagonists of the drama are the citizens; they act and their behavior enables the system to undergo transformation.

Few works in the modern public-administration literature are so firmly centered on knowledgeable, goal-directed citizen acts. Even much of the best work urging a more active citizenship—thought which is far removed from a customer orientation—is directed at agency employees and is primarily concerned with their role in facilitating citizen involvement. Louis Gawthrop tells administrators that a primary task is to "infuse the individual citizen with the character of citizenship and to provide the citizen with an ethical sense of purpose."[15] Eugene McGregor, Jr. argues that the administrator must sustain, encourage and spoon-feed the public.[16] Here the public is weak and needs help in learning its role. The protagonists are the agency managers who supply aid and affect a transformation.

The modern literature is much less oriented to analyzing citizen actions that originate outside administrative tutelage. Gawthrop and McGregor seem less likely than the bureau writers to believe large numbers of citizens capable of such actions. The bureau in its heyday would probably have agreed with Dwight Waldo's critique of Gawthrop:

> a civil servant should be a *servant*, that is an instrument or tool
> ... The idea ... that civil servants are going to instruct citizens
> in their citizenship role would strike most citizens as one or
> more of the following: impractical, presumptuous, humorous,
> outrageous.[17]

The bureau would want more emphasis placed on the citizen as actor. It was optimistic about the public's desire to get involved and its ability to make an impression on politics and administration. Perhaps no other group of American writers had such a positive perception of the citizen's intentions and capabilities. This optimism led the bureau to posit that active citizens are a prerequisite to improving public-agency performance. In this vision "it is the duty of the citizen quite as much as the duty of the officer to assume responsibility for the constructive side of government"[18]. Nobody has ever said that it is the duty of the customer quite as much as that of the manager to attend to the constructive side of business! The customer simply decides whether or not to buy certain products or services and in the public-sector even this freedom is often missing because the services are mandated for all citizens or those citizens who belong in a particular category.

Community

Another difference between the consequences of each metaphor is that when an agency views middle-class citizens as customers, no reason exists to think they will care whether the city delivers equal services to rich and poor. Each customer cares about his or her own needs. A person who buys a $50,000 automobile does not worry if the individual purchasing a $15,000 model has to put up with an inferior paint job. The essence of customer-firm relations is that cash talks. The person who has more money is supposed to have access to a wider array of products including most of those made with the finest craftsmanship.

Use of the customer metaphor elicits a picture of the middle-class citizen as shopper, an inherently individualistic role where each person gauges his or her own desires and does not care how the service provider treats those with lower incomes. This is why a key difference in the owner and customer models relates to the role of private-sector alternatives. The reinventing government paradigm assumes that it is proper for people who are unhappy with public services to seek education or security on the private market. The bureau castigates those who switch. Bruere writes

> The most inefficient citizen is one who sends his child to a private school *because* public schools are inefficient, who collects his own garbage *because* public collectors are unreliable, who paves his own street *because* a highway bureau is incompetent, or employs his own watchmen *because* police are undependable. (emphasis in the original)[19]

In the fall of 1994 controversy erupted in New York over a plan of residents in an affluent Manhattan neighborhood to levy $200 a year on the owners of co-ops and commercial properties and hire a private security force to patrol the area.[20] If residents are the New York City police department's customers, this plan makes sense. They have sampled the agency's services, consider them inadequate, and intend to move on and try an alternative provider. If residents are the department's owners, the plan is irrational; if these property owners believe service is inadequate, they should fight to make it better for everyone involved in *their* enterprise.

Customers do not need to have loyalty to any particular merchant; wealthy customers can find their own purveyors and leave the poor to cope with problems in a public education or police protection system. Only when citizens are viewed as owners, is the assumption made that they will try to fix the business rather than abandon it. The owner (and the owner alone) cares about the long-term health of the entire enterprise. The Bureau of Municipal Research could ask its predominately middle-class followers to monitor equal provision of safe schools and streets only because it alloted them an owner's role and assumed owners care about service delivery throughout the enterprise. The National Performance Review, on the other hand, asks each person to focus only on how new standards will affect his or her own service delivery; administrators assume that readers will take a customer's individualistic approach to benefits. In regard to community, citizen owners bear similarity to David Korten's "responsible citizens" who transcend individualistic cultural conditioning to think critically and constructively about the larger good of the societal enterprise.[21]

The two metaphors end by having drastically different consequences as Table 5.1 shows. They structure reality in variant ways. If we want to have a passive citizenry with each of its members approaching administrative questions from the point of personal interests, than the customer metaphor should be given wide publicity. If the vision of an active citizenry concerned with the public nature of public decisions sounds enticing, the owner metaphor should be brought to the foreground. Accepting one analogy without looking at the other allows partialistic assumptions about the citizen-agency relationship. The study of efficient citizenship offers a fuller picture of the possible range of agency-public relationships than appears from examining the reinventing government scenario alone. But key questions remain to be tackled: Is efficient citizenship practical? Can citizens assume a more active role?

Table 5.1
Customers and Owners: Two Orientations

Customers	Owners
Passive: responds to agenda set by others	Active: sets agenda
Meets individual needs	Meets needs of the enterprise

Efficient Citizenship and American Reality

The efficient citizenship model of action seems far removed from contemporary American reality. Our society does not do an adequate job of developing citizens who want to get involved in public-sector issues. Knowledge of and participation in America's political processes is low enough to justify speaking of "a massive state of civic illiteracy."[22]

Voting is generally a time limited, uncontroversial act of public involvement yet the decline in participation levels at the voting booth is among the most clearly documented trends in American politics since 1960. Only a little more than half the eligible people participate in presidential elections; less turnout exists for off-year congressional or local contests.[23]

Jury service is another traditional act of public involvement. The national no-show rate for individuals sent summonses for jury service currently stands at fifty-five percent.[24] This figure indicates that more people disregard the summons to serve than take advantage of the option to participate in the justice process.

Most citizens never take advantage of hearings and other opportunities to make their views known. By statute the California Energy Commission has a public advisor to tell the organization how to attract participation at hearings. Yet members of the public only attended fourteen of fifty-four open hearings in 1981 and five of twenty-three in 1982; at least half of the people who came to these events represented organized interest groups rather than concerned individuals.[25] A study of the California Coastal Commission found similar light participation.[26]

Camilla Stivers suggests that our society actually teaches people to regard citizenship as a waste of time[27]—a point of view that achieves credence from a recent Kettering Foundation study.[28] A seminal theme in focus groups with men and women across the nation was that these people saw themselves as politically impotent, as having lost control of the public agenda. Many people said they did not attend hearings because they did not believe that their participation would gain them genuine access to the system. They did not think politicians and administrators would listen to their comments. This psychological state predominated even though research shows that in some forums citizen participation has made a difference in the outcome of agency hearings.[29] In other words the psychological world view is generated by concentrating on that part of reality that supports a picture that locks them out and disregarding the aspects of reality that give room to hope that citizens can make a difference.

Most disturbing of all, some contemporary professionals question whether the public-in-general is intelligent enough to participate in community activity. Jury service has been open to citizens of all educational backgrounds for hundreds of years. Yet some modern lawyers suggest that juries lack "moral discipline" because they contain "unsophisticated, untrained, undisciplined" men and women. A panel of judges is proffered as an improvement.[30] Meanwhile, the chief judge of the United States Court of Appeals for the Seventh Circuit believes that civil-case juries should be discretionary with the bench because "[A]s American law and society become ever more complex, the jury's cognitive limitations will become ever more palpable and socially costly."[31] He labels it as an act of romanticizing to see average people as possessing deep enough wisdom to understand the facts in tort litigation.

Adopting this view does more than echo the Hanus-Moore-Greene notion that the public should not interfere in matters beyond its competence. It raises the notion to new heights because previous eras accepted the idea that citizen juries were essential to justice even if many jury members did not have extensive formal education. The seventh amendment to the constitution required juries in most civil cases at the end of the eighteenth century, an era when very few people had any technical training. It seems that at the same time this book is questioning the low citizen profile in the contemporary public sphere, other people are trying to reduce the citizen's role even further. These individuals think our political system restricts too few tasks to experts. They want technical expertise given a more prominent role in political decision making than it already has.

Is the possibility of efficient citizenship then a mirage? Are we better off forgetting about the owner model because while it may have theoretical interest it can never affect the real world? Dwight Waldo once said the bureau leaders believed most citizens were pure of heart and would rise to the challenge of public action.[32] Was this belief a total mistake, wishful thinking, or an example of extreme naivete?

Three reasons can be ventured for questioning the viability of the efficient citizenship concept. A look at the current participation patterns might lead a person to say active citizenship goes against human nature, it is inappropriate for our particular society although possibly viable elsewhere or it must fail because organized interests will strangle attempts at strong participation. Let us briefly sketch each argument, admit that it may be partially correct and propose nonetheless that even if each argument has some truth in it, still room remains to move towards a more owner-oriented model.

Human Nature

Some people argue that human nature precludes widespread participation. In this view people are seen as wanting to spend time in activities with tangible short-term payoffs. Active citizenship requires a certain degree of selflessness at least in the short run. In the long run it may lead to a better city for everyone but in this view the average citizen either refuses to worry about long-term contingencies or foists responsibility for improving the polity on others. This behavior of shunning active citizenship is regarded as perfectly natural. Concentrating on employment and home offers citizens a more efficient way of satisfying their own desires than does public-sector activity. A politics that requires citizens to spend long hours debating matters in the public interest is bound to fail because it places too great a burden on people's schedule and emotional resources.[33]

Citizen-owners have to learn to care about the success of an entire enterprise (the public service) rather than focusing solely on how a particular agency responds to their individual demands— although different citizen-owners may have variant definitions of what constitutes success. People who say human nature precludes this behavior believe that most people will never spend a significant part of their time working to meet the needs of others. They point to present behavior patterns to bolster their prediction. Even William Prendergast who as New York City comptroller supported the BMR, came to believe by the 1950s that Allen had overestimated the average citizen's interest in and aptitude for public affairs.[34]

Type of Society

Another argument is that active citizenship might have been a viable option in a small, homogeneous society but cannot work in a large, diverse polity such as our own.[35] Some people accept that active citizenship was the norm in eighteenth-century New England or in ancient Athens even though they cannot see their own acquaintances relishing intense levels of participation. For these people active citizenship seems suited to what they envision was a simpler time with fewer conflicts and less need for technical expertise. For them, efficient citizenship is an idea whose time has passed. Human nature allows it; our society does not. This argument is at the nub of the disdain some lawyers and judges have for juries. Lay citizens might have had the competence to ascertain facts in simpler times but not in our sophisticated society.

One of the ironies of this line of thought is that political scientists cannot agree on the optimal size and structure that facilitate participation. Some people argue that participation increases with multiple, overlapping jurisdictions and authority fragmented among diverse decision centers. Other scholars insist that small polities are the worst locus for participation because interest in local government is not high and the American population is extremely mobile.[36] It may be that some people gravitate more naturally to being active local citizens while others concentrate on national participation.

Interest-Group Opposition

A third argument is that political actors who benefit from apathy will successfully fight any attempt to enlarge the citizen's role. If people try to live up to their obligations, entrenched interests will minimize the usefulness of their efforts. The outcome of many political contests depends on who participates; to the extent that the rich or organized interests benefit from an apathetic public they will discourage active citizenship.

Allen believed in the importance of getting many citizens involved to counter lobbying by the rich; cynics may not be surprised that in 1914 the Rockefeller interests declined to fund his efforts and succeeded in minimizing their impact. You do not have to be a thoroughgoing cynic to predict that more people would respond in Cleveland's manner (by switching tack) rather than Allen's. At any rate, Allen's dedication to principle did not prevent his opponents from sabotaging efficient citizenship. As head of the underfunded Institute of Public Service he did not have the same platform to disseminate his message that had been available at the bureau.

The rich are not the only ones who stand to gain from limiting the public's role. Public administrators also may fail to welcome hordes of participating citizens if they view them as having a potentially destablizing affect on "their" agencies.[37] Bruere never explained how the police would respond to individuals checking up on the patrol's work habits. Allen found the education agency hostile to his attempts to get it to share information with the public.

Career officials have something to gain, at least in the short run, from restricting a large and variegated population from requesting yet another series of budget changes or organization charts. Citizen input can be costly to the administrator in time and the ability to reach closure. It can bring conflict into the open when the agency might prefer to rely on neutral expertise as the sole decision-making criterion.

The articles by Gawthrop and McGregor that were cited earlier attempt to change the behavior of recalcitrant officials by arguing that public employees must educate citizens for participation. But there is no reason to believe that administrator psyches are any more malleable than those of mass publics; it can be argued that it is human nature for administrators to guard their turf and take a short-run orientation to increased participation.

Rebuttals to efficient citizenship based on human nature, societal type, and interest-group opposition are not easy for a modern proponent of citizen ownership to dismiss. The empirical reality of low participation lends support to the case they seek to prove. What we must keep in mind in confronting such arguments is that even the bureau did not suggest that citizens donned an owner's mantle in all circumstances. The BMR saw that the urbanites in its era were apathetic. Indeed, if most city dwellers had lived up to bureau ideals in 1906, no need would have existed for an efficient-citizenship campaign.

The Allen-Bruere-Cleveland literature argues that citizens will act as owners when the proper education and information are available to them. Education will provide the disposition and capacity to act selflessly. Information will bridge geographic boundaries and make technical subjects understandable to lay audiences. Fortified with the proper disposition and knowledge citizens will brave the special interests that seek to limit their roles.

It is hard for a contemporary observer to be quite as sanguine as the bureau about this scenario. The BMR argued that as soon as people realized that free public-school dental clinics were the only way to make certain poor children had good teeth then even "the most conservative will not hesitate long" to endorse their funding.[38] Modern readers are likely to chuckle at this naivete and explain that a devoted foe of government expenditures will either never be convinced that clinics are necessary or will proffer a counterargument explaining why their installation is too expensive even if required to ensure the health of poor children.

In addition, the modern observer can learn about the bureau's campaign for citizen-ownership and how it was thwarted. This story which was obviously not available as a guiding narrative in 1907 highlights the strength and determination of those interests that are threatened by active citizen participation. It suggests that these interests will not simply sit back and welcome increased involvement. Conflict is likely to attend the dissemination of proposals that actually increase the number of people participating in the public sphere and the intensity of their involvement.

If change could only come from people who possessed the bureau's optimism, then the idea of efficient citizenship would be doomed. But you do not need the bureau's transcendent belief in the truimph of a pure-hearted citizenry to say that some shift in the direction of more efficient citizenship is possible. Even if better education and information exchange alone are insufficient to get most people to assume the active monitoring role envisioned by the BMR, they do seem necessary to increasing interest or participation to any significant degree. A society in which most people limited their participation to voting in local elections and accepting their first jury summons would fall far short of bureau expectations but would still be far higher in citizen involvement than our own.

One can be a skeptic about the possibility or desirability of achieving the bureau's scenario in full and still say that it seems reasonable that efficient, responsive government can never emanate solely from reinventing institutions; somehow we have to get citizens involved. The bureau founders were extremely optimistic about the prospects for change. A modern skeptic who favors a more active citizenry is likely to be less optimistic but willing to venture the following proposal: "Look, we are in trouble to the extent that human nature or the complexities of our society preclude us from reinventing ourselves and taking an ownership role. I do not know how far human nature or society will allow change in this direction but let us improve education for citizenship and information exchange and see how far these changes take us. We will know better how to gauge the potential boundaries of human behavior after people are educated for active citizenship and have access to the information they need to participate."

After all, while some current commentators argue that human nature precludes active participation, other thinkers have considered political involvement the essence of human identity. Aristotle, for example, postulated that people were by nature political animals; he saw participation in the civic sphere as crucial to the happiness of the individual.[39]

Such bottom-line disagreements on human psychology exist because no one can define the essence of human nature outside of a social setting; all commentators base their hypotheses on actions that occur in organized societies. Nothing that happens in 1960s–1990s America can define human identity; it can simply show how this nature reacts to the social arrangements in our particular polis. Vary the education, change the information channels and you may deflect what our society considers "normal" participation patterns.

In addition, even if the societies we know are less amenable to intense participation than a city-state, this does not mean that in a polity that is even more technologically sophisticated than our own citizenship would wither even further. The impact of size and technological sophistication may be curvilinear rather than ongoing in a never-ending straight line of citizenship dimunition. A trend in the 1990s is for companies to flatten hierarchies and give middle- and lower-level employees more decision-making capabilities. Empowering people to make decisions at work may increase their sense of efficacy and communication skills. It may lead them to see organizational decision making as an interesting and viable activity for them. These gains in turn may persuade workers to desire more access to public-sector decision-making opportunities and encourage public involvement. Changes in industrial structure may facilitate advances in active citizenship in the years to come.[40]

The skeptic's attitude centers on a time-directed prescription for renewal: first change the underlying conditions relative to education and information and then see where human nature takes the polity. Certainly both areas still need improvement in ways that we will now examine.

Citizenship Education

Education for citizenship is more important for owner than customer models because efficient citizens have to learn to care about the success of the public sector in the entire community rather than simply about whether agencies deliver the goods to them. They must appreciate that the polity benefits when significant numbers of its inhabitants assume a community-centered orientation.

Useful citizenship education has cognitive, skills and psychological dimensions. The cognitive component affords students a basic core of knowledge. They are exposed to the nation's central political traditions and to the way government is organized and operates.

The skills component relates to acquiring communication abilities with an emphasis on "know how" rather than "know that." Students are taught how to write letters to officials and how to speak and listen at meetings.

The third component centers on fashioning a psychological identity to undergird action. Much of this dimension occurs sub rosa without explicit labels as to purpose. Children learn the joys of participation by taking part in in-class team projects or extracurricular activities such as newspapers, school bands, or sports. They learn to accept the obligations of citizenship when they see teachers whom they admire extoll those who get involved.

Much of the popular criticism of education centers around the school's inability to give graduates an adequate knowledge base. Certainly high school seniors have dramatic lacuna in their fact bank when less than sixty percent know that the Bill of Rights guarantees freedom of religion or that the Declaration of Independence affirms the right to life, liberty, and the pursuit of happiness.[41] This lack of knowledge is a problem for active citizenship as owners should understand something about the history and working assumptions of their enterprises.

But political scientists argue that education increases participation for two reasons outside the cognitive (know-that) dimension. The important relationships are that it increases people's communication skills and their sense of duty and efficacy.[42] Communication skills matter because the costs of participation are lower for people who are comfortable speaking and writing in public; such individuals are more likely to participate because they find it less taxing to make their voices known. A sense of duty and a sense of efficacy are crucial because their possessers are more likely to believe they have an obligation to participate and that their actions count. These are important psychological hurdles that must be crossed before people bother to get involved. Few people participate when involvement seems an exercise in futility.

Proponents of better education for citizenship have to care then about skill acquisition and psychological identity—two areas where the educational system is weak. Contemporary social studies classrooms stress passive textbook reading; they do not afford students sufficient practice writing and speaking about policy concerns.[43] Most assessments test memory of facts rather than the ability to analyze material or apply it to solve contemporary problems.[44] Few teachers would take the risks associated with Allen's idea of having students develop their skills by devising ways of improving their own education. No wonder that a majority of a sample of Illinois high-school seniors said that civics courses did not increase their interest in government or public affairs.[45]

Many schools have a hidden curriculum of cynical realism whose message is that democratic ideals are constantly violated through greed and incompetence. Students are implicitly told that the savvy, hip citizen realizes he or she cannot make a difference; only the fool gets involved.[46] Those in the know resign themselves to an imperfect system and get on with the crucial private areas of life. The late Ernest Boyer, a former president of the Carnegie Foundation for the Advancement of Teaching, noted that with citizenship education of this sort "America runs the risk of drifting unwittingly into a new kind of dark age, a time when specialists control the decision-making process."[47]

Information Exchange

Our situation in regard to the availability of information on agency performance is very different from that of the BMR era. Almost all public organizations prepare reports on their activities; the federal and state Freedom of Information Acts (FOIA) mandate that a wide variety of in-house papers are available to anyone who wants to read them. Nonprofit interest groups generate additional reports which are widely available.

Yet simple existence of data does not necessarily produce information exchange; for that to happen, people have to want to expose themselves to the data. In our society few people seek access to the information that is available. Most FOIA requests emanate from businesses seeking indicators on government assessment of their products or their competitors'. Comparatively few come from public-interest groups or individuals.[48]

The paucity of civically-oriented requests may occur for two reasons. First, people may not be aware of what is available. Citizens have to know about the existence of documents to request them and few people understand the wide variety of topics on which the government prepares reports. Individuals often do not even know for which benefits they are eligible. Many low-income residents, for example, are unaware of the qualified Medicare beneficiary program where Medicaid pays deductibles for Medicare payments.[49] It is not unreasonable to assume, therefore, that an even greater number of citizens know nothing either of the FOIA's existence or of their right to ask for public-agency documents. This is why the bureau urged the importance of advertizing government publications and hearings.[50]

Second, too many documents are prepared in a user-hostile manner that makes people shy away from wanting to see their contents. Precisely because information is a political resource it is often withheld, manipulated or distorted. Administrators who prepare government reports may consciously or subconsciously work in a manner to make the issues barely comprehensible or irrelevant to citizen concerns by framing discourse in the jargon of some professional speciality.[51] The bureau argued that agencies in its day did not present data in a useful format for citizens who wanted to monitor organizational performance and make suggestions. Studies of local government budgets and reports in the late 1970s and in our own decade conclude that most are still ill-suited for use by people who intend to make agencies toe the mark; most still lack any comparative performance data that could be used to question the direction of specific bureaus or programs.[52]

The use of jargon has probably escalated since 1914 if only because of the proliferation of professions with their attendant schools and special vocabularies. Too many government reports are written in gobbledygook, a language characterized by excessive jargon and verbal runaround. The public advisor to California's Energy Commission argues that the reason few people attend commission hearings is because the documents under discussion are too complex for laypeople to understand.[53] The civil servants writing these reports do not seem to agree with Allen that the results of all government investigations should be transmitted in a form comprehensible to the average citizen.[54] Some of these administrators may prefer to restrict the discussion to those people who share a particular professional language and its assumptions; they see that this limits the strange, provocative questions that will be asked.

The upshot of these problems is that people still do not believe they have enough information to participate meaningfully in public debates.[55] More fundamentally, many individuals do not understand what they are missing by not having access to comprehensible information. Education has to supply the motive for them to demand this type of data and to seek it out—and education for citizenship is weak. As in the bureau era, the people least likely to pursue information are the poor, which means that such participation as exists will often be skewed to the middle class. Neither in terms of providing proper education nor fostering genuine information *exchange* does our society facilitate active citizenship. Whether we view this as a weakness depends on our preferred model of citizen-agency relationship. Do we envision the public as customers or owners of their government? If we envision citizens as owners, then it is a problem that the proprieters lack the psychological and informational resources to mind their own businesses! Improvements in education and information exchange are vital to any movement that wants to increase citizen interest and participation in the public sphere.

CHAPTER 6

STRATEGIES
FOR REFORM

Proponents of reinventing government articulate concrete strategies to create entrepeneurial administrators who gauge the reactions of citizen-customers and use administrative skills to improve client satisfaction. A recent appraisal argues that the Gore report has changed the culture of government, by simplifying rules and procedures and requiring every federal agency to inaugurate pilot reinvention projects within a specific period.[1] Those people who argue that increased citizen involvement is also a prerequisite to improving government must offer equally concrete steps for reinventing an active citizenry. This is the only way for their proposal to get a serious hearing.

The bureau assumed that education and information are the foundations for building an active citizenry. The first element supplies the desire and the second the means for participation. Any implementation plan for reinventing citizenship has to focus on these entities. The analysis below explores a suggestion for improvement in each area. The first concern is with education which is crucial to producing citizens with a taste for public involvement. The suggestion is to expand on a directed variant of service-learning which some colleges and high schools have already started to implement.

The second concern is with information. The problem is how to motivate people so that they care to look at data, some of which have been available in one form or another for quite a while. The strategy is municipal-government production of a more user-friendly variant on the annual report corporations distribute to keep stockholders informed. The proposal not only shows how to get information to the public but how to use the transmittal process as a vehicle for increasing citizen deliberation. The reporting process itself sparks an opportunity for two-way communication and public involvement in setting parameters for future reports. Implementing these ideas is one way of opening the process of citizen reinvention.

Education

While people receive their citizenship education in numerous places including families, houses of worship, and workplaces, the American political system has always assigned the school a key role in imparting cognitive information about government and feelings about national identity. Any approach to increasing a citizen-owner orientation has to include steps to make schools more reliable agents for producing people with a taste for public-sphere involvement. This means sharpening the ability of the schools to develop their students' communication skills and produce adults who believe that being an active citizen is worthwhile.

To some readers the school may seem an odd choice of intervention point because most socialization research shows only a small correlation between the civics courses students take and their political knowledge.[2] But these studies merely underscore that the heart of education for democracy does not lie in conventional coursework. Much better correlations appear between student participation in school activities and subsequent political orientation. Path analysis data from a national socialization panel study of young Americans shows that participating in extracurricular activities is an important agent of political learning. The experience young people gain by such involvement has a greater affect on whether they become involved in election campaigns or attend community meetings than does their parents' socioeconomic status or political participation.[3]

Active citizenship is not something one learns simply by reading a textbook. The key to producing active citizens is to involve students in community-oriented activities. By practicing service in the public interest they learn something about what the public-interest dimension of citizenship entails. They develop the communication skills necessary for comfortable participation in the public sphere. Allen and Bruere understood what was needed when they argued that students had to leave their desks and use academic skills such as writing, recording and measuring to ameliorate actual community problems such as tenement deficits. They preached education that benefited both the community and the development of the student.

Under the rubric of service learning American educational institutions today are experimenting with instruction that also moves academic skills into a community setting. This vision implies a marriage between experiential education and class-based analysis of whatever students discover in the field.[4] Intellectual abilities are honed while students contribute to the solution of real-world problems through projects tailored to meet specific community needs. As a complement to field placement, classes engage in critical reading and discussion about community, citizenship, rights and democracy. These readings orient students to the civic dimension of service work, while at the same time ongoing field experiences are used to analyze and critique the readings.

If we consider civic literacy as important as scientific or mathematical literacy, then no theoretical consideration should impede requiring all students to participate in directed service projects during high school and college.[5] As longitudinal research shows that political attitudes can and do change both during and after adolescence[6], secondary and postsecondary education are appropriate venues to help students abstract values and norms from experience and integrate them to create an approach to public life. Fortunately, at both the collegiate and secondary levels, important voices are speaking up for service learning.

Colleges and Universities

The growth of service learning at the collegiate level can be seen in the 1985 establishment of Campus Compact, a coalition of over four hundred college and university presidents committed to helping students improve civic participation through public-service involvement.[7] The 1993 passage of the federal National and

Community Trust Act temporarily facilitated development of service-learning opportunities by awarding approximately nine million dollars in 1994 to colleges that make service part of the student experience.[8]

A recent analysis of the impact of service courses gives room for guarded optimism that they can influence student attitudes at least in the short run. Data collected at Rutgers University indicate that students enrolled in service learning courses had a stronger sense of civic capacity than their peers enrolled in comparison offerings.[9] Student journals included such comments as "A citizen must play an active role in his or her community," and "service is part of my civic responsibility."[10]

While it is difficult to pinpoint which aspect of service learning enhances civic orientation, one salient feature may be participant recognition that individual actions make a difference at least in a restricted sphere. Two students who completed service projects at New Jersey Institute of Technology made these comments:

> The things I learned about the community service work and community service agency that I didn't know before is how important my contribution was. I always thought that I really had nothing to offer to anyone or that anyone would accept something besides my money. (senior majoring in architecture)

> One aspect of my work there that brought me the most satisfaction was the feeling that all my reports were taken very seriously and promptly acted upon. The negative aspects of working for a large corporation such as impersonal environment and feelings that my work is not appreciated were absent. (sophomore majoring in computer and information science)[11]

These students began the term with a feeling of alienation not unlike the one that was so prevalant among adults in the Kettering Foundation sponsored focus groups discussed in chapter 5. They thought those with whom they worked would ignore their suggestions. Their actual experience led them to reconceptualize their potential efficacy which could change the way they approach a multitude of political situations. With their new attitudes they are more likely to offer opinions at hearings and participate in policy-deliberation forums. Trust and a sense of efficacy are needed to bring people into the public arena and these are the very goods that the service-learning experience can provide.

Community-based projects are not limited to courses that bear a formal "service learning" designation. An American government course at Wayne State University, for example, requires a political activity component where students work on voter registration drives and related projects.[12] Although the professors do not use the service-learning label, students receive many of the same educational benefits. The key is to provide class members with work that benefits the community and time to reflect as a group on the civic implications of their projects.

High School

Unfortunately, collegiate service learning by itself cannot create an inclusive citizenry of concerned owners. This solution leaves out all those citizens who quit school after high school graduation. Indeed, if service learning succeeds in raising civic consciousness among baccalaureate holders while the rest of the population maintains its current lethargic participation levels, the reform would have the ironic impact of further skewing participation towards the middle classs and thus contributing towards a marginalization of blue-collar workers and the poor.

The way to raise a broad population's civic consciousness is to bring service learning to the secondary level where it can influence people preparing for a range of occupations. The most heartening movement on this front occured in 1983 when the Carnegie Foundation for the Advancement of Teaching recommended that every high-school student complete a service requirement of not less than thirty hours per year.[13]

Mandating service as part of the secondary school's academic curriculum serves both to legitimize and democratize it by showing that it is not a form of noblesse oblige but rather a duty and obligation imposed on all people. Poorer students take part as often as richer ones, a state of affairs that might not ensue if the projects were optional and conflicted with hours normally used to take on a part-time job.

A 1983 study of eight high school programs found an increase in participant's sense of responsibility to the larger community.[14] As happens at the collegiate level, students see that goal-directed action produces accomplishments for the community and this whets their appetite for additional involvement. An appetizer course of participation leads naturally to trying a main dish.

Ernest Boyer tells of a high school class that successfully lobbied its city council to change a neighborhood street name.[15] The student's victory should jump start an increase in their sense of efficacy facilitating a willingness to get involved in another context. At least it is less likely that adolescents such as these who see that their actions matter will grow up to mirror the alienation of the men and women in the Kettering focus groups.

It is no accident that modern proponents of service learning rationalize the innovation in terms reminiscent of those people used before 1915 to explain the need for a citizen-owner orientation. Two proponents of service learning at the college level write that they can envision a hypothetical student enrolling because he or she believes, "I cannot flourish unless the communities to which I belong flourish, and it is my (enlightened) self-interest to become a responsible member of those communities."[16] How similar this sentiment is to that of a large print blurb in the *Efficient Citizen*, "My town's affairs are my affairs; its welfare is my welfare. I cannot separate myself from my town's affairs and my town's welfare. I and my town are so closely related."[17] The similarity of tone underscores that service learning is a useful method to increase citizens' perceptions of themselves as active, community-minded owners.

Information

Improvements in citizen-government information exchange are discussed today almost entirely in terms of technological solutions. According to this view past generations lacked the information to participate, at least partly, because of an inadequate number of transmission channels. An array of new media—personal computers, electronic mail, cable television, telephone networks—will increase the amount of data available and the time and space in which they can be received.[18] This fusion of computers and communications will further empower the many to participate in "making policy" in domains to which the few, with their moth-eaten monopolies of knowledge, will have to yield more and more access.[19]

New channels will open the gates to a wider audience seizing the chance to use multiple information sources.

Nobody should underestimate technology's ability to change the information landscape especially in the long run. The number of electronically available documents can only increase in the next several decades as will the number of households possessing computer hardware and information-processing skills.

The availability of more information will not mean that this resource will be used. The discussion in chapter 5 emphasized that many individuals are alienated from the political process; these people believe that their participation cannot count. With this mindset they are unlikely to buy access to politically-relevant information as they would not see any need for it.

Sophisticated transmission channels by themselves will not motivate people to pursue subjects that have no interest for them. A prior need is to convince the audience that data about public activities have pragmatic potential. First give people a reason to expose themselves to data. When they believe public-sector information can help them maneuver through their own agendas, that is the time to discuss whether they want to hook into sophisticated systems to transmit or exchange information.

The focus on high tech strategies is also inappropriate at this time because such solutions exacerbate differential access based on income and education. Already the middle-class is more likely to participate in the public sphere. Putting citizenship on-line unilaterally advantages those people whose educational backgrounds stress computer usage. Households with the largest array of electronic equipment will find access easier and more enjoyable than will those possessing fewer gadgets.

In the long run computers may become as ubiquitous as televisions but at present they are hardly as common in poverty-level as in middle-class neighborhoods. The Big Three commercial, general interest, on-line services—CompuServe, American Online and Prodigy—have only between five and six million subscribers combined, a figure that pales besides the listeners commanded by the major television channels. Nobody knows exactly how many people use the Internet but individuals who do not work for large organizations must pay companies called access providers to get on-line or enter through links provided by the Big Three. Again, access is limited for the poor.[20]

The focus at this time should be on delivering information to citizens at their homes in a format equally available to almost all people where the delivery process itself is a prelude to deliberation by interested members of the public on how to structure future reports.[21] The entity providing the information should be the government under the understanding that public entities should give their owners at least as much operational and financial information as corporations provide shareholders. Too often agencies consider public-information provision a low-priority item and do not extend to their owners the information that government mandates large companies provide theirs.[22]

Each year publicly held corporations mail stockholders a report relating corporate activities and providing financial disclosure. Prompted by Securities and Exchange Commission rules companies share information on sales and earnings, assets, capital expenditures, depreciation and the state of various corporate operations. Unfortunately, many shareholders barely leaf through their reports; again we find that simply disclosing information is insufficient to sustain interest. But perhaps local governments can build on the idea of a report mailed to shareholders and improve on the product so that it engages an audience that does not begin by perceiving its contents as affecting primary interests.

One positive aspect of company reports is that they are mailed to recipients; stockholders do not have to guess what type of information is available and request it. (Thus company reports are very different than the National Performance Review's suggested consolidated annual financial report for citizens which does not contain a provision for mass-mailings.[23] We know that if people have to request this document from the Treasury Department, most will never see it.)

A corresponding weakness, however, is that company reports are not tailored to individual needs. Every stockholder receives the same document. Inevitably this leaves some shareholders drowning in unwanted financial statistics while others are upset by the lack of detail.

Local governments should adopt the corporate mailing strategy while building choice into the process of document selection. This entails having a repetoire of materials and giving citizens some ability to choose the pieces they want after they have been exposed to an introductory booklet that explains the uses to which the information might be put. The heart of this strategy is that it tries to tailor the information each household receives to its capacity to use it and that it contains provisions for interested members of the public to critique the reports and help construct more useful ones in the future. A potential plan is outlined below.

A Three-Step Reporting System

In this plan the city generates three levels of reports each with increased detail. These include city, agency, and bureau presentations.

THE CITY REPORT

The city report is mailed once a year to all households and gives information on operating-agency performance. A motivation section opens the booklet explaining why people should care about the rest of the material. The remainder of the narrative identifies goals for key operating agencies along with accomplishments, problems encountered, solutions tried and any need to revise plans. The purpose is to spotlight the most significant information on administrative goals and activities using both qualitative and quantitative achievement measures.

Readability is key to this document's success. The format must be so clear that people unfamiliar with a given operation can follow descriptions of its activities without difficulty. Pictorial aids such as charts, graphs, and statistical maps can yield visual information to support narratives. The tone should be honest and constructive; if a program suffers a major setback, this fact is reported with ample consideration to causes and effects and recommendations for change. Modern agency communicators may want to revive the Bureau's "vulgar" device of using brightly-colored paper to attract immediate attention.

Even so, the prospect for mass readership is not large if the performance measures themselves are esoteric or mundane.[24] What are wanted are indicators that allow comparisons which are meaningful to the audience and put the community's pride at stake. The average scores of school children are more interesting when presented against those of other students from similar socio-economic backgrounds. The rate of injury at recreation centers in City X is useful for evaluative purposes if compared to rates in jurisdictions with much lower or higher incidences of accidents.

Near the beginning and end, the document indicates that readers who want further information on any topic can send for agency reports, each one dealing with a separate function. A prepaid postcard with a check-off space for each request is attached.

AGENCY REPORTS

Prepared once a month, agency reports assemble greater detail on a given function such as education, fire, police or sanitation. Each report contains an agency's mission statement, selected qualitative and quantitative performance indicators, and narrative analysis of one or two critical issues in the area. The end of the document informs readers that further information on any of the issues discussed is available in a series of bureau reports. A prepaid postcard is attached.

Each month, approximately a week after the city mails these reports, high-level agency executives hold a series of meetings with citizen readers in the different urban neighborhoods to discuss the contents. One topic is always the performance criteria themselves. The audience is asked to suggest other indicators it would like to see in the city and agency narratives; a system exists for incorporating citizen suggestions into future bulletins. (The procedures for incorporation might vary by function.)

Other people who have written about active citizenship have seen the need to create some kind of neighborhood assembly to encourage the development of citizen competence.[25] Benjamin Barber, for example, urges assemblies where people "assess the local impact of regional and national bills, explore ideological stances in the absence of pressures from special-interest groups, and introduce new questions of interest to the neighborhood."[26]

Two problems with developing assemblies have been (1) how to get entrenched interests to allow the establishment of forums which may shift the balance of political power and (2) how to get people to believe that attending such assemblies would be an appropriate activity for them, that their attendance and deliberation could influence urban policy, if such assemblies were formed. Without such conviction people simply will not commit time. Any forum will be empty unless participants see that their participation has political consequences.

The report-oriented meetings could grow into such neighborhood forums for active citizenship by self-selected individuals with interests in different public activities. The original report-oriented meetings would have the leadership of agency functionaries who would assume that they could guide the deliberations. Thus it would be easier to get public-official support for such meetings than for neighborhood assemblies without public-administrator participation. They would be a viable format for interaction because the people who attended would set the criteria presented in subsequent city and agency reports. Administrators could not simply ignore suggestions but would have to act on them at least in the context of the reporting system itself. Seeing their influence on the reporting system would increase citizen efficacy which would make it more likely that these people, at least, would participate in other forums. The participants in the report-oriented meetings would want to form genuine neighborhood assemblies. Their new found efficacy would make them formidable contenders against special interests that tried to stop them from establishing deliberative assemblies where interested citizens would meet to deliberate policy issues.

BUREAU REPORTS

The third-tier reports supply the greatest amount of detail and statistical analysis of quantitative performance indicators. Having this information would put a citizen recipient on a knowledge par with administrators who had day-to-day access to internal files at least as far as statistical/quantitative data are concerned. Initial demand for these papers is likely to be quite low; requests may grow, however, if people attend the meetings generated by the agency reports and wish to probe more deeply into topics they discuss in that venue.

Politics and Expenses

Introducing the reports is not without its political perils. As noted earlier, administrators may be reluctant to share comparative data because they do not want to publicize programmatic failures. Some bureaucrats may cringe at the prospect of report-generated forums and an energized, participating citizen body.

Ideally, involved citizens would be the vehicle for forcing reporting but until they see the benefits of information few citizens will take the initiative in a campaign to provide elaborate mailings. Thus, any drive for enacting this system would have to be spearheaded by the small group of people who intuitively understand the use of performance-based reports and press for them by stressing their link to service improvement.

Opponents of the three-tier reporting system will probably contend that its cost is prohibitive. They may allege that the mailings seem to depress efficiency since they simply report progress rather than contribute directly to line accomplishments. But a cost-conscious attitude to public reports neglects the important dimensions of responsiveness and accountability. The public-sector cannot be responsive without citizen input; citizens cannot provide input without sufficient information to evaluate agency performance. Those people who accept that citizen involvement is crucial to producing a government that works better will conclude that the cost of the reports is necessary precisely because it contributes to providing better services. The mailings are not simply a public relations frill but rather help further programmatic missions which can never be approached efficiently without citizen aid.

Allen once objected to a state law that exempted New York City from filing specified reports because the city was understaffed. He said, "That's as undemocratic as can be. It's against efficiency."[27] People who believe that internal change alone can improve governmental performance might say the law supports efficiency by forcing administrators to concentrate on their line tasks rather than public communication. With a citizen-owner model, however, efficiency is impossible without information exchange.

Recently, the New York City school system began to build on this idea by having children bring home report cards on their schools to spark parental involvement. The three-page annual reports (which are also used in other jurisdictions) allow parents to compare teacher experience, overcrowding, suspension rates, and other variables in their school and the system as a whole. The report cards do not lead to a forum for parent/administrator deliberation nor do they provide different information packets based on the needs of individual home units but they do represent a trend towards bringing information to the public rather than asking people to find the data they need to get involved. Ramon Cortines, the New York City school chancellor who started the practice, noted that the report-card information had always been available to people willing to wade through layers of bureaucracy but now more parents would use it since it was brought to them.[28] The same change in transmission practice must occur in other functions. Information must become readily available to people with a wide variety of educational backgrounds.

Conclusions

The twentieth-century has seen innumerable attempts to improve federal, state and local government performance through structural change. From the days of President Taft to the National Performance Review various task forces, commissions and committees have touted internal arrangements that their progenitors were certain would produce efficient government. These recommendations have led agencies to shift management systems repeatedly over time. Every era has its privileged arrangements. At one point the efficiency Rx is centralization; later, agencies are told improvement requires decentralization. The only constant is that no suggestion brings long-term satisfaction. No matter what solutions jurisdictions try, eventually presidents, governors, and local executives return to the task-force drawing board with fresh pleas to find a way to make government work better.

The time has come to realize that structural change alone will never guarantee effective government. An involved, active citizenry is a co-prerequisite for significant change. No managerial shift can close the trust deficit that so many alienated Americans feel today vis-à-vis their government. The way to close this deficit is by increasing citizen involvement in the public sphere, getting a wide variety of people to participate in agenda setting and policy implementation. We have to return to the notion that public-sector efficiency does not exist in principle without responsiveness to the community—that no public action can be efficient if it does not respond to community desires—and that government simply cannot be responsive to a passive citizenry. Responsiveness requires citizen involvement.

The concept that citizen involvement is crucial to creating a government that works better means that at least part of the onus for any current derelictions falls squarely on the public's shoulders rather than those of political figures and administrators. An apathetic public sets the stage for a distant, preoccupied bureaucracy.

Current reform proposals do not include a wake-up call to the public to assume its obligations since customers have no obligations to the enterprise from which they buy products and services. Indeed, reinventing government's popularity may stem in part from the reassuring and complacent message it sends the American people. The National Performance Review implies that government's problems emanate solely from anachronistic legislation and bureaucratic procedures. Reform requires political figures to hustle and get their houses in order. Citizens can sit back comfortably in their rocking chairs and watch government improve to meet their expectations.

In discussing welfare and crime, politicians often bandy about the phrase "personal responsibility" but somehow this notion is off limits in analyzing efficiency. Nobody says that in a democracy the population as a whole may very well get the government services it deserves, that politicians and administrators cannot gauge what citizens want unless many members of the public turn proactive and help to carve out a satisfying public agenda. Instant popularity will not accrue to the politician or administrator who admits that the public-sector needs citizen oversight, that service levels will not shift significantly until people experience a sense of personal responsibility for bettering the public enterprise.

The National Performance Review lists numerous action steps that agencies must take for service renewal. Those people who believe that improvement requires efficient organizations *and* efficient citizens cannot be optimistic that pursuing agency-generated steps alone will produce a satisfactory government. For that to occur citizen-owners have to draw up action plans for themselves. They have to ask the old question, "Am I minding my own business?"

NOTES

Chapter 1

1. See David Osborne and Ted Gaebler, *Reinventing Government* (Reading, Massachusetts: Addison Wesley, 1992) and Executive Office of the President, National Performance Review, *From Red Tape to Results: Creating a Government that Works Better and Costs Less* (Washington, D.C.: U.S. Government Printing Office, 1993).

2. *From Red Tape to Results*, p. 3.

3. Frederick Cleveland chaired the commission; political scientists Frank Goodnow and W.F. Willoughby served as commissioners. United States President's Commission on Economy and Efficiency, *Message of the President of the United States on Economy and Efficiency in the Government Service* (Washington, D.C., 1912).

4. Louis Brownlow chaired the committee; political scientists Luther Gulick and Charles Merriam served as commissioners. United States President's Committee on Administrative Management, *Report of the Committee with Studies of Administrative Management in the Federal Government* (Washington, D.C.: U.S. Government Printing Office, 1937).

5. Frederick Taylor, *Shop Management* (New York: Harper and Row, 1947 [originally printed 1903]), p. 63.

6. Harrington Emerson, *Efficiency as a Basis for Operation and Wages* and *Twelve Principles of Efficiency*, both published by (New York: Engineering Magazine Press, 1912) and Henri Fayol, *General and Indus-*

trial Management, trans. Constance Storrs (London: Sir Isaac Pittman, 1949). A fuller development of the history of the principles literature appears in Hindy Lauer Schachter, "The Role of Efficiency in Bureaucratic Study," in *Handbook of Bureaucracy*, ed. by Ali Farazmand (New York: Marcel Dekker, 1994).

7. Martin Schiesl, *The Politics of Efficiency* (Berkeley: University of California Press, 1977).

8. (New York: Institute of Public Administration).

9. Chapters 2–4 reference this literature in detail.

10. *The Efficient Citizen* published 1913–1914 by the Municipal Service Bureau. Available New York Public Library.

11. William Munro, *Principles and Methods of Municipal Administration* (New York: Macmillan, 1915), pp. 3–4 and 6.

12. William Capes, *The Modern City and Its Government* (New York: E. P. Dutton, 1922), pp. 2 and 14.

13. See, for example, Jesse Burks, "Efficiency Standards in Municipal Management," *National Municipal Review*, 1 (July 1912), 364–371.

14. This analysis is based on the most widely used textbooks and readers in the introductory MPA course. In the order of their use these books include: Richard Stillman, II, *Public Administration: Concepts and Cases*, 4th ed. (Boston: Houghton Mifflin, 1988); Jay Shafritz and Albert Hyde, *Classics of Public Administration*, 2nd ed. (Chicago: Dorsey, 1987); George Gordon, *Public Administration in America*, 3rd ed. (New York: St. Martin's Press, 1986); Nicholas Henry, *Public Administration and Public Affairs*, 4th ed. (Englewood Cliffs, New Jersey: Prentice-Hall, 1988); Felix Nigro and Lloyd Nigro, *Modern Public Administration*, 7th ed. (New York: Harper and Row, 1989); David Rosenbloom, *Public Administration*, 2nd ed. (New York: Random House, 1989); and Grover Starling, *Managing the Public Sector*, 3rd ed. (Chicago: Dorsey, 1986). For an analysis of how textbook use in this course was compiled see Hindy Lauer Schachter, "Graduate Education in Public Administration: The Introductory Course," *International Journal of Public Administration*, 16, 1 (1993), 1–13.

15. *Administrative Behavior* (New York: Free Press, 1947).

16. Vincent Ostrom, *The Intellectual Crisis in American Public Administration* (University, Ala: University of Alabama Press, 1974). See also Robert Golembiewski, "A Critique of "Democratic Administration" and Its Supporting Ideation," *American Political Science Review*, 66 (December 1977), 1488–1507.

17. *From Red Tape to Results*, p. 3.

18. Al Gore, Jr., "The New Job of the Federal Executive," *Public Administration Review*, 54 (July/August 1994), 317–321.

19. Heinrich Boll, "The Man With the Knives" in *Great German Short Stories*, ed. by Stephen Spender (New York: Dell, 1960).

20. *The New York Bureau of Municipal Research* (New York: New York University Press, 1966).

21. See, for example, Alice Stone and Donald Stone, "Early Development of Education in Public Administration" in *American Public Administration: Past, Present, Future*, ed. by Frederick Mosher (University, Alabama: University of Alabama Press, 1975).

22. See, for example, Terry Cooper, "Citizenship and Professionalism in Public Administration," *Public Administration Review*, 44, special issue (March 1984), 143–149, Donald Critchlow, *The Brookings Institution, 1916–1952: Expertise and the Public Interest in a Democratic Society* (Dekalb: Northern Illinois University Press, 1985), pp. 17–18, or Camilla Stivers, "Settlement Women and Bureau Men: Constructing a Usable Past for Public Administration," *Public Administration Review*, 55 (Nov./Dec. 1995), 522–529.

23. See particularly chapter 6; James Thompson and Vernon Jones, "Reinventing the Federal Government: The Role of Theory in Reform Implementation," *American Review of Public Administration*, 25 (June 1995), 183–199 assert that David Osborne drafted the federal report.

24. *From Red Tape to Results*, p. i.

25. Ibid., pp. 47–48.

26. Del Borgsdorf, " 'The Local Citizen: Voter, Taxpayer and Customer" in *Effective Communication: A Local Government Guide* ed. by Kenneth Wheeler (Washington, D.C.: International City/County Management Association, 1995), 33–46.

27. Louis Gerstner, Jr., Roger Semerad, Dennis Doyle and William Johnston, *Reinventing Education: Entrepeneurship in America's Public Schools* (New York: Dutton, 1994).

28. James Swiss, "Adapting Total Quality Management (TQM) to Government," *Public Administration Review*, 52 (July/August 1992), 356–362.

29. For a discussion of the use of metaphors see Murray Edelman, *The Symbolic Uses of Politics* (Urbana: University of Illinois Press, 1985),

George Lakoff and Mark Johnson, *Metaphors We Live By* (Chicago: University of Chicago Press, 1980), Martin Landau, "On the Use of Metaphors in Political Analysis," *Social Research*, 28 (Autumn 1961), 331–353, and Eugene Miller, "Metaphor and Political Knowledge," *American Political Science Review*, 73 (March 1979), 155–170.

30. Danny Balfour and William Mesaros, "Connecting the Local Narratives: Public Administration as a Hermeneutic Science," *Public Administration Review*, 54 (November/December 1994), 559–564.

31. Harlan Cleveland, "The Twilight of Hierarchy: Speculations on the Global Information Society," *Public Administration Review*, 45 (January/February 1985), 185–195.

32. H. George Frederickson, "The Seven Principles of Total Quality Politics . . .," *Public Administration Times*, 17 (1), p. 9.

33. This issue is discussed in Ronald Moe, "The "Reinventing Government" Exercise: Misinterpreting the Problem, Misjudging the Consequences," *Public Administration Review*, 54 (March/April 1994), 111–122 and David Rosenbloom, "Have an Administrative Rx? Don't Forget the Politics," *Public Administration Review*, 53 (November/December 1993), 503–507.

34. John DiIulio, Jr., Gerald Garvey and Donald Kettl's, *Improving Government Performance: An Owner's Manual* (Washington, D.C.: Brookings, 1993) does contain the word "owner" in the title but the book itself is concerned with explicating the customer metaphor.

35. Stephen Toulmin, *Human Understanding* (Princeton: Princeton University Press, 1972), vol. 1, pp. 267–268.

36. Ibid., p. 220.

37. Alasdair Roberts, "Demonstrating Neutrality: The Rockefeller Philanthropies and the Evolution of Public Administration, 1927–1936," *Public Administration Review*, 54 (May/June 1994), 221–228.

38. See the discussion in Lori Verstegen Ryan and William Scott, "Ethics and Organizational Reflection: The Rockefeller Foundation and Postwar "Moral Deficits," 1942–1954," *Academy of Management Review*, 20 (April 1995), 438–461.

39. Roberts, p. 222.

40. See, for example, Sheldon Wolin, "Democracy: Electoral and Athenian," and J. Peter Euben, "Democracy Ancient and Modern," both in

PS: Political Science and Politics, XXVI (September 1993), 475–477, and 478–481, respectively.

41. Hannah Arendt, *On Revolution* (New York: Viking, 1963), p. 119.

42. Benjamin Barber, *Strong Democracy: Participatory Politics for a New Age* (Berkeley, California: University of California Press, 1984), p. 151.

43. See, for example, Martin Schiesl, *The Politics of Efficiency* and Robert Wiebe, *The Search for Order, 1877–1920* (New York: Hill and Wang, 1967).

44. See, for example, Henry Bruere, "Public Utilities Regulation in New York," *Annals*, 31 (May 1908), 535–551.

45. Abraham Flexner, *The Educational Activities of the Bureau of Municipal Research of New York: A Report to the General Education Board*, 1914. Rockefeller Foundation Archives, General Education Board Papers, Box 274, Folder 2859.

46. William Allen, *Universal Training for Citizenship and Public Service* (New York: Macmillan, 1917), pp. 34–35.

Chapter 2

1. For an account of the reform movement see Richard Hofstadter, *The Age of Reform: From Bryan to FDR* (New York: Alfred Knopf, 1959).

2. Frederick Mosher, *Democracy and the Public Service* (New York: Oxford University Press, 1968).

3. See Jane Dahlberg, *The New York Bureau of Municipal Research* (New York: New York University Press, 1966).

4. William Allen, "Reminiscences" (1949/1950), vol. 1, p. 159. Unpublished manuscript in Oral History Collection, Columbia University.

5. The account of Allen's early life comes from "Reminiscences".

6. Ibid., pp. 46–47.

7. Ibid., p. 46.

8. Ibid.

9. New York City Board of Education, "Report No. 2 of the Special Committee of Five" (Feb. 1904). Unpublished report available at Depart-

ment of Special Collections, Millbank Memorial Library, Teachers College, Columbia University.

10. Walter Drost, *David Snedden and Education for Social Efficiency* (Madison, Wisconsin: University of Wisconsin Press, 1967), pp. 86–87.

11. New York City Board of Education, *Journal of the Board of Education of the City of New York* (New York: Board of Education, 1904), vol. 1, pp. 763–766.

12. Ibid., pp. 230–231.

13. New York City Finance Department, *Report of an Investigation Concerning the Cost of Maintaining the Public School System* (New York: Martin Brown, 1904/1905) and Board of Education, *Report No. 2 of the Special Committee of Five*.

14. This account comes from 1) Association for Improving the Condition of the Poor, *Communication in Behalf of Vacation and Night Schools, Recreation Centers and Popular Lectures* (Jan. 9, 1905). Appeal to the Board of Education. Available New York Public Library; and 2) Letter from William Allen to Abraham Flexner, Feb. 5, 1914. Rockefeller Foundation Archives, General Education Board Papers, Box 274, Folder 2857.

15. *Journal of the Board of Education*, pp. 165–166.

16. Allen to Flexner, Feb. 5, 1914.

17. "Work To Be Done by the Institute for Municipal Research" (1905). Typewritten manuscript available in Citizen Union Papers, City Committee File, Box K–1, Manuscript Collection, Columbia University. See, also, letter from Frederick Cleveland to members of the Industrial Relations Commission, Feb. 2, 1915. Rockefeller Foundation Archives, General Education Board Papers, Box 274, Folder 2858.

18. An account of some of his activities appears in Wallace Sayre and Herbert Kaufman, *Governing New York City: Politics in the Metropolis* (New York: Russell Sage, 1960), p. 497 and William Prendergast, "Reminiscences" (1948–1951), vol. 2, p. 163. Available Oral History Collection, Columbia University.

19. Cleveland to Industrial Relations Commission, Feb. 2, 1915, p. 2.

20. Bureau of City Betterment. *The Police Problem in New York City* (New York: Citizens Union, 1906).

21. Cleveland to Industrial Relations Commission, Feb. 2, 1915.

22. Charles Beard, "Philosophy, Science and Art of Public Administration," unpublished address to the Governmental Research Association, Princeton, New Jersey, Sept. 8, 1939. Available at the New York Public Library.

23. Cleveland to Industrial Relations Commission, Feb. 2, 1915, p. 2.

24. "Not Moved by Rockefeller," *New York Times* (July 19, 1914), sec. II, p. 8.

25. Robert Binkerd, "Reminiscences" (April/May 1949), p. 11. Available Oral History Collection, Columbia University.

26. Prendergast, "Reminiscences", vol. 6, pp. 948–950.

27. Drost, *David Snedden and Education for Social Efficiency*, pp. 97–98.

28. Letter from Abraham Flexner to Wallace Buttrick, April 10, 1914. Rockefeller Foundation Archives, General Education Board Papers, Box 274, Folder 2858.

29. Allen, "Reminiscences", p. 483.

30. "Work To Be Done by the Institute for Municipal Research."

31. Allen's fund-raising is discussed in his "Reminiscences" and in Cleveland to Industrial Relations Commission, Feb. 2, 1915. His pre-eminent role in raising money from the Rockefellers can be seen in the various letters in Rockefeller Foundation Archives, Record Group III2D, Folder 5. For examples of the work as intermediaries undertaken by John, Jr. and Starr Murphy see letter from John Rockefeller, Jr. to John Rockefeller, Sr., Jan. 7, 1909 and letter from Starr Murphy to John Rockefeller, Jr., May 18, 1911. Rockefeller Foundation Archives, Record Group III2D, Folder 5 and 10, respectively.

32. "Dr. Allen Attacked by Research Chief,"" *New York Times* (Feb. 4, 1914), p. 7.

33. The document signed by the Trustees is Bureau of Municipal Research, *Purposes and Methods of the Bureau of Municipal Research* (New York: Bureau of Municipal Research, 1907).

34. Bureau of Municipal Research, *Business Methods of New York City's Police Department*.

35. For example, Henry Bruere, "The Future of the Police Arm from an Engineering Standpoint," *American Society of Mechanical Engineers*

Transactions, 36 (1914), 535–547 and William Allen, *Efficient Democracy* (New York: Dodd, Mead and Co., 1907), pp. 184–185.

36. Allen, "Reminiscences", vol. 1, p. 159.

37. "Bruere, A Chicago Don Quixote," *Tammany Times* (Feb. 13, 1909), p. 9. Rockefeller Foundation Archives, Record Group III2D, Folder 5.

38. Dahlberg, *The Bureau of Municipal Research*, p. 12.

39. Letter from William Maxwell to Abraham Flexner, Dec. 11, 1913, pp. 3–4. Rockefeller Foundation Archives, General Education Board Papers, Box 274, Folder 2856.

40. Bureau of Municipal Research, *Making a Municipal Budget* (New York: Bureau of Municipal Research, 1907). For the reasons for the department's request see Edward Sait, "Research and References Bureaus," *National Municipal Review*, 2 (Jan. 1913), 48–56.

41. Frederick Cleveland, *Chapters on Municipal Administration and Accounting* (New York: Longmans, Green and Co., 1909), p. 77.

42. Martin Schiesl, *The Politics of Efficiency* (Berkeley, California: University of California Press, 1977), p. 100.

43. Herman Metz, *Cost of Government of the City of New York with an Analysis of the Budget for the Year 1909* (New York: Finance Department, Dec. 1908). Available Department of Special Collections, Teachers College, Columbia University, Board of Education Pamphlets, Box 73.

44. Bureau of Municipal Research, *Business Methods of New York City's Police Department* (New York: Bureau of Municipal Research, April 1909).

45. Luther Gulick, *The National Institute of Public Administration* (New York: National Institute of Public Administration, 1928).

46. Charles Goodsell, "Charles A. Beard, Prophet for Public Administration," *Public Administration Review*, 46 (March/April 1986), 105–107 (quote on p. 106).

47. Bureau of Municipal Research, *Report on a Survey of the Department of Public Safety, Pittsburgh* (New York: Bureau of Municipal Research, 1913).

48. See, for example, Allen, *Efficient Democracy*, p. 67 or Frederick Cleveland, "Municipal Ownership as a Form of Governmental Control," *Annals*, 35 (1906), 359–370.

49. See, for example, Henry Bruere, *The New City Government* (New York: D. Appleton and Co., 1912), p. 13.

50. *Efficient Citizenship*, no. 180, August 1909. The Bureau's unpublished Efficient Citizenship postcards and circulars are available at the New York Public Library. This series of mailings is discussed in more detail in chapter 3.

51. Bureau of Municipal Research and Training School for Public Service, *Efficiency and Next Needs of St. Paul's Health Department* (New York: Bureau of Municipal Research, 1913).

52. Bureau of Municipal Research, *A Report on the Division of Child Hygiene, Department of Health* (New York: Bureau of Municipal Research, 1911), p. 6.

53. Bureau of Municipal Research, " A Report on the Homes and Family Budgets of 100 Patrolmen," in *Police in America* (New York: Arno Press and New York Times, 1971). The original report was drafted by Genevieve Beavers, a Training School graduate, in 1913.

54. See, for example, Frederic Howe, *The Modern City and Its Problems* (New York: Scribner's, 1915), pp. 330–331 and Myrtile Cerf, "Bureaus of Public Efficiency," *National Municipal Review*, 2 (Jan. 1913), 39–47.

55. Bureau of Municipal Research, *Help-Your-School Surveys: Waterbury Public School and Classroom Instruction in St. Paul* (New York: Bureau of Municipal Research, 1913), p. 16.

56. William Prendergast, "Efficiency through Accounting," *Annals*, 41 (May 1912), 43–56.

57. Frederick Cleveland, *Organized Democracy* (New York: Longmans, Green and Co., 1913), p. 79.

58. Frederick Cleveland, "The Need for Coordinating Municipal, State and National Activities," *Annals*, 41 (May 1912), 25–39 (quote on p. 27).

59. Henry Bruere, "Efficiency in City Government," *Annals*, 41 (May 1912), 1–22.

60. Bruere, *New City Government*, pp. 1–2.

61. Executive Office of the President, National Performance Review, *From Red Tape to Results: Creating a Government that Works Better and Costs Less* (Washington, D.C.: U.S. Government Printing Office, 1993), p. 2.

62. William Allen, "Instruction in Public Business," *Political Science Quarterly*, 22 (1908), 604–616.

63. Gulick, *The National Institute of Public Administration*.

64. George Graham, *Education for Public Administration* (Chicago: Public Administration Service, 1941), p. 135.

65. Paul Van Riper, "Luther Gulick on Frederick Taylor and Scientific Management," *Journal of Management History*, 1, 2 (1995), 7–9 and Dahlberg, *The New York Bureau of Municipal Research*, p. 129.

66. Gulick, *The National Institute of Public Administration*, pp. 60–63.

67. Leonard White, *Trends in Public Administration* (New York: McGraw-Hill, 1933), p. 260.

68. Edward Fitzpatrick, "What is Civic Education?" *National Municipal Review*, 5 (April 1916), 278–282 (quote is on p. 279).

Chapter 3

1. See, for example, Henry Bruere, *The New City Government* (New York: D. Appleton and Co., 1912) or Frederick Cleveland, *Chapters on Municipal Administration and Accounting* (New York: Longmans, Green and Co., 1909) and *Organized Democracy* (New York: Longmans, Green and Co., 1913), pp. 99–112.

2. *Chapters on Municipal Administration and Accounting*, pp. 346–347.

3. See, for example, Cleveland, *Organized Democracy*, p. 454 or Bruere, *The New City Government*, p. 107.

4. Cleveland, *Organized Democracy*, pp. 438–443.

5. Ibid., pp. 99–112 and Frederick Cleveland, "The Need for Coordinating Municipal, State and National Activities," *Annals* (May 1912), 23–39.

6. William Allen, "Reminiscences", 1949/1950, vol. I, pp. 99–100. Unpublished manuscript in Oral History Collection, Columbia University.

7. Bruere, *The New City Government*, p. 121.

8. William Allen, "Efficiency in City Government," *City Club Bulletin*, 2 (April 22, 1908), p. 127. Quoted in Martin Schiesl, *The Politics of*

Efficiency (Berkeley, California: University of California Press, 1977), pp. 115–116.

9. *Chapters on Municipal Administration and Accounting*, pp. 263–264.

10. Bureau of Municipal Research, *Administrative Methods of the City Government of Los Angeles, California* (Los Angeles: Municipal League of Los Angeles, 1913), pp. 6, 7 and 16.

11. David Snedden and William Allen, *School Reports and School Efficiency* (New York: Macmillan, 1908) and Cleveland, *Chapters on Municipal Administration and Accounting*, pp. 268–275.

12. Snedden and Allen, *School Reports and School Efficiency*, pp. 5–6.

13. Letter from William Maxwell to Abraham Flexner, Dec. 11, 1913. Rockefeller Foundation Archives, General Education Board Papers, Box 274, Folder 2856.

14. John Tildsley, "School Reports as They Are: A Rejoinder," in Bureau of Municipal Research, *School Progress and School Facts* (New York: Bureau of Municipal Research, July 1909), p. 19.

15. William Allen, "School Reports as They Are" in Bureau of Municipal Research, *School Progress and School Facts* (New York: Bureau of Municipal Research, 1909).

16. *New City Government*, pp. 288–290.

17. William Allen, *Civics and Health* (Boston: Ginn and Co., 1909), p. 29 and *Women's Part in Government* (New York: Dodd, Mead and Co., 1911), pp. 95 and 185–186.

18. *Municipal Research*, June 20, 1914. Available Institute of Public Administration, New York.

19. Richard Battistoni, *Public Schooling and the Education of Democratic Citizens* (Jackson, Miss.: University Press of Mississippi, 1985), p. 89.

20. William Allen, *Universal Training for Citizenship and Public Service* (New York: Macmillan, 1917), pp. 50–51. An analysis of the Gary plan appears in Raymond Callahan, *Education and the Cult of Efficiency* (Chicago: University of Chicago Press, 1962), chapter 6.

21. *New City Government*, p. 122.

22. Allen, *Universal Training for Citizenship*, p. 77.

23. "New York's Budget Exhibit," *Charities and the Commons*, 21 (October 10, 1908), p. 74.

24. Allen, *Reminiscences*, vol. 1, p. 159.

25. Lent Upson, "The Value of Municipal Exhibits," *National Municipal Review*, 4 (January 1915), 65–69.

26. Laity League, Social Service Conference, "Honesty, Economy, Efficiency." Election pamphlet available Citizens Union Papers, Box W–4, Columbia Manuscript Collection, Columbia University.

27. Allen, "Reminiscences," vol. 1, p. 97.

28. Leo Rowe, *Problems of City Government* (New York: D. Appleton and Co., 1908), p. 191.

29. This miscellaneous material is available at the New York Public Library.

30. Allen, "Reminiscences," vol. 1, p. 161.

31. *Municipal Research* (December 1913), p. 4. Available at the Institute of Public Administration, New York.

32. Allen, *Women's Part in Government*.

33. Ibid., pp. 16–17.

34. Allen, *Universal Training for Citizenship*, p. 35.

35. Allen, *Civics and Health*, chapter 23.

36. William Allen, *Efficient Democracy* (New York: Dodd, Mead and Co., 1907), p. vii.

37. Allen, *Women's Part in Government*, p. 56.

38. Bureau of Municipal Research, *Report on a Survey of the Department of Public Safety, Pittsburgh* (New York: Bureau of Municipal Research, June-July 1913), p. 76. Available at the New York Public Library.

39. Allen, "Reminiscences."

40. Allen, *Universal Training for Citizenship*, p. 87.

41. Henry Bruere, "America's Unemployment Problem," *Annals*, 61 (September 1915), 11–23.

42. Allen, *Efficient Democracy*, pp. 198–199.

43. *Municipal Research* (October 25, 1913). Available at the Institute of Public Administration, New York.

44. *Municipal Research* (November 15, 1913).

45. *Municipal Research* (October 11, 1913).

46. Eda Amberg and William Allen, *Civic Lessons from Mayor Mitchel's Defeat* (New York: Institute for Public Service, 1921).

47. Bruere, *New City Government*, p. 396.

48. Sidney Verba et al. "Citizen Activity: Who Participates? What Do They Say?" *American Political Science Review*, 87 (June 1993), 303–318.

49. See, for example, the reform social-work journal *Charities and the Commons*, for the 1900–1915 period.

Chapter 4

1. Bureau of Municipal Research, *Digest of the School Inquiry* (New York: Bureau of Municipal Research, 1913).

2. Paul Hanus, *School Efficiency: A Constructive Study Applied to New York City* (Yonkers, New York: World Book Co., 1913) and *Adventuring in Education* (Cambridge, MA: Harvard University Press, 1937).

3. See the analysis in David Tyack and Elisabeth Hansot, *Managers of Virtue: Public School Leadership in America, 1820–1980* (New York: Basic Books, 1982) and Frederick Wirt and Michael Kirst, *Schools in Conflict* (Berkeley, California: McCutcheon, 1982), chapter 1.

4. Charles Eliot, "City Government by Fewer Men," in *Charles W. Eliot: The Man and His Beliefs*, ed. by William Neilson (New York: Harper and Brothers, 1926).

5. Wirt and Kirst, *Schools in Conflict*.

6. Quoted in "The New York School Inquiry," *National Municipal Review*, 2 (January 1913), 88–93.

7. Ernest Moore, "My Relation to the New York School Investigation," n.d. Unpublished memorandum available in Rockefeller Foundation Archives, Record Group III2D, Folder 9.

8. Hanus, *Adventuring in Education*, pp. 176–182. Hanus refers to his antagonist as "Mr. X, a BMR director," but it is clear from the context that he refers to Allen.

9. Bureau of Municipal Research, *Digest of the School Inquiry*.

10. Henry Bruere, "Public Utilities Regulation in New York," *Annals*, 31 (May 1908), 535–551.

11. Ernest Moore, *How New York City Administers Its Schools* (Yonkers, New York: World Book Co., 1913), p. 91.

12. Diane Ravitch, *The Great School Wars: New York City, 1805–1973* (New York: Basic Books, 1974), pp. 193–195.

13. Committee on School Inquiry, "Special Report of the Committee on School Inquiry of the Board of Estimate and Apportionment," in *Report of Committee on School Inquiry Board of Estimate and Apportionment* (New York: Board of Estimate and Apportionment, 1912), vol. 3, 459–509 and Lewis Mayers, "The New York School Inquiry," *National Municipal Review*, 3 (April 1914), 327–339.

14. Quoted in Mayers, "The New York School Inquiry."

15. Quoted in "Special Report of the Committee on School Inquiry," vol. 3, p. 477. Report cites the letter as from Moore to Mitchel, Sept. 3, 1912.

16. Letter from Jerome Greene to Paul Hanus, November 11, 1912; letter from Hanus to Greene, November 12, 1912. Rockefeller Foundation Archives, Record Group III2D, Folder 9.

17. Letter from Jerome Greene to Charles Howland, president of the Public Education Association, April 16, 1913. Rockefeller Foundation Archives, Record Group III2D, Folder 9.

18. Paul Hanus, unpublished memorandum, June 15, 1913, p. 2. Rockefeller Foundation Archives, Record Group III2D, Folder 6.

19. Letter from Jerome Greene to Paul Hanus, November 11, 1912, p. 4.

20. Letter from Paul Hanus to Jerome Greene, Nov. 12, 1912. Rockefeller Foundation Archives, Record Group III2D, Folder 9.

21. Letter from Jerome Greene to Ernest Moore, March 10, 1913. Rockefeller Foundation Archives, Record Group IIID, Folder 9.

22. Committee on School Inquiry, "Special Report of the Committee on School Inquiry of the Board of Estimate and Apportionment," vol. III, p. 461.

23. Frank Goodnow and Frederick Howe, "The Organization, Status and Procedure of the Department of Education, City of New York," in *Report of Committee on School Inquiry*, vol. 3, 1–316.

24. *Efficient Citizenship*, no. 579, "Are Those Who Employ Educational Experts Justified in Demanding Facts to Support Generalizations?" Available New York Public Library.

25. *Efficient Citizenship*, no. 604, "Address of Thomas Churchill," Feb. 1913, p. 3. Available New York Public Library.

26. Letter from Ernest Moore to Jerome Greene, November 19, 1912. Rockefeller Foundation Archive, Record Group III2D, Folder 9.

27. Letter from Charles Eliot to Jerome Greene, November 15, 1912. Rockefeller Foundation Archives, Record Group III2D, Folder 9.

28. Letter from Jerome Greene to Ernest Moore, March 10, 1913. Rockefeller Foundation Archives, Record Group, III2D, Folder 9.

29. Memorandum by Jerome Greene on a letter from William Allen, November 13, 1912, p. 2. Rockefeller Foundation Archives, Record Group III2D, Folder 8.

30. Letter from Jerome Greene to Paul Hanus, March 13, 1913. Rockefeller Foundation Archives, Record Group IIID, Folder 9.

31. Letter from Starr Murphy to William Allen, November 29, 1912. Rockefeller Foundation Archives, Record Group III2D, Folder 6.

32. Letter from Paul Hanus to Jerome Greene, March 12, 1913. Rockefeller Foundation Archives, Record Group III2D, Folder 9.

33. Memorandum by Jerome Greene concerning the Bureau of Municipal Research, March 17, 1913, p. 4. Rockefeller Foundation Archives, Record Group III2D, Folder 6.

34. Letter from Jerome Greene to William Allen, October 9, 1913, pp. 1–2. Rockefeller Foundation Archives, Record Group RG 1.1, Box 14, Folder 147.

35. Letter from William Allen to John Rockefeller, Jr., May 9, 1913. Rockefeller Foundation Archives, Record Group III2D, Folder 6.

36. Letter from John Rockefeller, Jr. to Abraham Flexner, May 9, 1913. Rockefeller Foundation Archives, General Education Board Papers, Box 274, Folder 2856.

37. An overview of Flexner's career appears in Franklin Parker, "Abraham Flexner, 1866–1959," *History of Education Quarterly*, 2 (Dec. 1962), 199–209.

38. Letter from William Allen to Abraham Flexner, May 5, 1913. Rockefeller Foundation Archives, General Education Board Papers, Box 274, Folder 2856.

39. Letter from William Allen to John Rockefeller, Jr., June 19, 1913. Rockefeller Foundation Archives, Record Group III2D, Folder 10.

40. "Memorandum of Correspondence between Dr. Allen, of the Bureau of Municipal Research and Mr. John D. Rockefeller, Jr. regarding investigation of the educational work of the Bureau," n.d. Rockefeller Foundation Archives, General Education Board Papers, Box 274, Folder 2856.

41. Ibid.

42. Letter from Paul Hanus to Abraham Flexner, December 23, 1913. Rockefeller Foundation Archives, General Education Board Papers, Box 274, Folder 2856.

43. Parker, "Abraham Flexner."

44. See, for example, letter from Abraham Flexner to B. Tinker, superintendent of Waterbury, Connecticut schools, January 19, 1914 or letter from Edward Mandel, principal of P.S. 188B, New York City, to William Allen, January 19, 1914. Rockefeller Foundation Archives, General Education Board Papers, Box 274, Folder 2857.

45. Letter from B. Tinker to H. L. Brittain, May 6, 1913. Rockefeller Foundation Archives, General Education Board Papers, Box 274, Folder 2857.

46. Abraham Flexner, *The Educational Activities of the Bureau of Municipal Research of New York*. Report to the General Education Board, February 1914, p. 19. Rockefeller Foundation Archives, General Education Board Papers, Box 274, Folder 2859.

47. Letter from Starr Murphy to John Rockefeller (no specification of whether recipient is John, Jr. or John, Sr.), February 16, 1914. Rockefeller Foundation Archives, Record Group III2D, Folder 6.

48. Letter from Henry Pritchett to Abraham Flexner, April 10, 1914. Copy available in William Allen's Papers, Manuscript Collection, Columbia University.

49. Association for Improving the Condition of the Poor, *Communication in Behalf of Vacation and Night Schools, Recreation Centers and Popular Lectures* (Jan. 9, 1905). Available New York Public Library.

50. R. Fulton Cutting, *Regarding the Educational Activities of the Bureau of Municipal Research and Training School for Public Service*, April 4, 1914. Rockefeller Foundation Archives, Record Group III2D, Folder 11.

51. William Allen, "Reasons Why Mr. Allen Believes that Mr. Rockefeller's Conditional Offer of Support to the New York Bureau of Municipal Research Should Not be Accepted." Remarks presented to BMR Board of Trustees, May 11, 1914. Copy available in New York Public Library.

52. "Directors Fall Out in Research Bureau," *New York Times*, July 18, 1914, p. 14.

53. Letter from R. Fulton Cutting to Jerome Greene, November 24, 1914. Rockefeller Foundation Archives, Record Group RG 1.1, Box 14, Folder 147.

54. Memorandum from Abraham Flexner, February 4, 1915. Rockefeller Foundation Archives, Record Group RG 1.1, Box 14, Folder 148 and "Directors Fall Out in Research Bureau."

55. Irene Rubin, "Early Budget Reformers: Democracy, Efficiency and Budget Reforms," *American Review of Public Administration*, 24 (September 1994), 229–251.

56. "Directors Fall Out in Research Bureau."

57. "Municipal Research," *New York Times*, July 20, 1914, p. 6.

58. Letter from Frederick Cleveland to members of the Industrial Relations Commission and accompanying "Statement of Facts," February 2, 1915. Rockefeller Foundation Archives, General Education Board Papers, Box 274, Folder 2858.

59. Letter from John Rockefeller, Jr. to Charles Coffin, August 7, 1914. Rockefeller Foundation Archives, Record Group III2D, Folder 6.

60. "Directors Fall Out in Research Bureau."

61. Letter from R. Fulton Cutting to Jerome Greene, November 24, 1914.

62. See, for example, letter from Frederick Cleveland to Abraham Flexner, May 28, 1915, Rockefeller Foundation Archives, General Educa-

tion Board Papers, Box 274, Folder 2858, and to Jerome Greene, October 8, 1914, Record Group RG 1.1, Box 14, Folder 147.

63. Letter from R. Fulton Cutting to Starr Murphy, April 7, 1916 and from Murphy to Cutting, April 18, 1916, Rockefeller Foundation Archives, Record Group III2D, Folder 6. Cutting gradually became less interested in supporting the new-style Bureau. By the early 1920s after the organization had changed its name to the National Institute of Public Administration he had become a minor figure among its donors. Letter from Raymond Fosdick of the Rockefeller Foundation to W. S. Learned of the Carnegie Corporation, Jan. 30, 1923. Available Carnegie Corporation Files, Grant Files, Box no. 183. Manuscript Collection, Columbia University.

64. Edward Fitzpatrick, "What Is Civic Education?" *National Municipal Review*, 5 (April 1916), 278–282 (quote on p. 279).

65. Letter from William Allen to John Rockefeller, Jr., January 17, 1918. Rockefeller Foundation Archives, Record Group III2D, Folder 11.

66. William Allen, "The Budget Amendment of the Maryland Constitution," *National Municipal Review*, 6 (July 1917), 485–491. The debate is analyzed in Rubin, "Early Budget Reformers."

67. Many items from this series are in the Rockefeller Foundation Archives, Record Group III2D, Folder 11.

68. Record Group III2D, Folder 11.

69. Letter from William Allen to John Rockefeller, Jr., June 29, 1925. Rockefeller Foundation Archives, Record Group III2D, Folder 11. Raymond Fosdick affixed the handwritten note.

70. William Allen, "Reminiscences" (1949/1950), Unpublished manuscript available in Oral History Collection, Columbia University, vol. 1, p. 127.

Chapter 5

1. Martin Landau offers this saying in "On the Use of Metaphor in Political Analysis," *Social Research*, 28 (Autumn 1961), 331–353.

2. W. F. Willoughby, *Principles of Public Administration with Special Reference to the National and State Governments* (Baltimore: Johns Hopkins Press, 1927), p. 6.

3. Bonnie Mani, "Old Wine in New Bottles Tastes Better: A Case Study of TQM Implementation in the IRS," *Public Administration Review*, 55 (March/April 1995), 147–158.

4. James Swiss, "Adapting Total Quality Management (TQM) to Government," *Public Administration Review*, 52 (July/August 1992), 356–362.

5. Robert Denhardt, *The Pursuit of Significance: Strategies for Managerial Success in Public Organizations* (Belmont, CA: Wadsworth, 1993), p. 79.

6. Paul Light, "Partial Quality Management," *Government Executive*, 26 (April 1994), 65–66.

7. Executive Office of the President, National Performance Review, *Putting Customers First: Standards for Serving the American People* (Washington, D.C.: U. S. Government Printing Office, 1994), p. 2.

8. Larry Lane and Gary Marshall, "Reinventing OPM: Adventures, Issues and Implications." Unpublished paper presented at the American Society for Public Administration Conference, July 1995.

9. Charles Goodsell, *The Case for Bureaucracy*, 2nd ed. (Chatham, New Jersey: Chatham House Publishers, 1985), 29.

10. Theodore Poister and Gary Henry, "Citizen Ratings of Public and Private Service Quality: A Comparative Perspective," *Public Administration Review*, 54 (March/April 1994), 155–160.

11. David Osborne and Ted Gaebler, *Reinventing Government* (Reading, MA: Addison Wesley, 1992).

12. Charles Goodsell, "The Grace Commission: Seeking Efficiency for the Whole People?" *Public Administration Review*, 44 (May/June 1984), 196–204.

13. Henry Bruere, *The New City Government* (New York: D. Appleton and Co., 1912), pp. 102–106.

14. Frederick Cleveland, *Organized Democracy* (New York: Longmans, Green and Co., 1913), p. 127.

15. Louis Gawthrop, "Civic, Civitas and Civilitas: A New Focus for the Year 2000," *Public Administration Review*, 44, special issue (March 1984), 101–107 (quote on p. 104).

16. Eugene McGregor, Jr., "The Great Paradox of Democratic Citizenship and Public Personnel Administration," *Public Administration Review*, 44, special issue (March 1984), 126–132.

17. Dwight Waldo, "Response," *Public Administration Review*, 44, special issue (March 1984), 107–109 (quote on p. 108).

18. Frederick Cleveland, *Chapters on Municipal Administration and Accounting* (New York: Longmans, Green and Co., 1909), p. 352.

19. Henry Bruere, "Efficiency in City Government," *Annals*, 41 (May 1912), 1–22 (quote on p. 21).

20. Thomas Lueck, "Business Districts Grow at Price of Accountability," *New York Times* (Nov. 20, 1994), pp. 1 and 46.

21. David Korten, *Getting to the 21st Century: Voluntary Action and the Global Agenda* (West Hartford, CT: Kumarian Press, 1990), p. 107.

22. James Chesney and Otto Feinstein, "Making Political Activity a Requirement in Introductory Political Science Courses," *PS: Political Science and Politics*, 26, 3 (1993), 535–538 (quote on p. 535).

23. See, for example, the analysis in Paul Abramson and John Aldrich, "The Decline of Electoral Participation in America," *American Political Science Review*, 76 (Sept. 1982), 502–521.

24. Richard Posner, "Juries on Trial," *Commentary*, 99 (March 1995), 49–52.

25. Michael Reagen and Lynn Fedor-Thurman, "Public Participation: Reflections on the California Energy Policy Experience," in *Citizen Participation in Public Decision Making*, ed. by Jack DeSario and Stuart Langton (Westport, CT: Greenwood Press, 1987), 89–113.

26. Judy Rosener, "Making Bureaucracy Responsive: A Study of the Impact of Citizen Participation and Staff Recommendations on Regulatory Decision Making," *Public Administration Review*, 42 (July/August 1982), 339–345.

27. Camilla Stivers, "The Public Agency as Polis: Active Citizenship in the Administrative State," *Administration and Society*, 22 (May 1990), 86–105.

28. Harwood Group, *Citizens and Politics: A View form Main Street America* (Dayton, Ohio: Kettering Foundation, 1991).

29. In some situations individual citizens who come to hearings seem to be able to influence outcomes; in other situations they have no discernible influence. A three-year study of the California Coastal Commission found light participation but those people who came to hearings influenced the commissioners' final decisions. (Rosener, "Making Bureaucracy Responsive . . .") A study of hearings on the General Revenue Sharing program found no statistically significant impact of citizen participation. (Richard Cole and David Caputo, "The Public Hearing as an Effective Citizen Participation Mechanism," *American Political Science Review*, 78 (June 1984), 404–416). The difference in impact might depend on the issues involved or on the personalities of the citizens and administrators at each hearing. More research is needed on which variables affect citizen influence.

30. S. Ezra Austern, "Surely, We Can Improve on Trial by Jury," *New York Times* (Dec. 31, 1994), p. 24.

31. Posner, "Juries on Trial," p. 52. To put this suggestion into operation would require changing the seventh amendment to the constitution which guarantees a jury trial in most civil cases.

32. Dwight Waldo, *The Administrative State* (New York: Ronald Press, 1948), pp. 16–17.

33. See, for example, Robert Dahl, *Modern Political Analysis* (Englewood Cliffs, New Jersey: Prentice-Hall, 1963) or *Who Governs?* (New Haven, Ct: Yale University Press, 1960). See also Shelley Burtt, "The Politics of Virtue Today: A Critique and a Proposal," *American Political Science Review*, 87 (June 1993), 360–368.

34. William Prendergast, "Reminiscences" (1948–1951), vol. 6, p. 950. Unpublished manuscript avilable in the Oral History Collection, Columbia University.

35. An analysis of this argument appears in J. Peter Euben, "Democracy Ancient and Modern," *PS: Political Science and Politics*, 26 (Sept. 1993), 478–481 and Stivers, "The Public Agency as Polis."

36. See, for example, the discussion in Vincent Ostrom, *The Intellectual Crisis in American Public Administration* (University, Ala: University of Alabama Press, 1974) and W. E. Lyons and David Lowery, "Governmental Fragmentation Versus Consolidation: Five Public Choice Myths About How to Create Informed, Involved and Happy Citizens," *Public Administration Review*, 49 (Nov./Dec. 1989), 533–543.

37. See Mary Kweit and Robert Kweit, "The Politics of Policy Analysis: The Role of Citizen Participation in Analytic Decision Making," in *Citizen Participation in Public Decision Making*, ed. by Jack DeSario and Stuart Langton (Westport, Ct: Greenwood Press, 1987), 19–38 and Ray MacNair, Russell Caldwell and Leonard Pollane, "Citizen Participants in Public Bureaucracies: Foul-Weather Friends," *Administration and Society*, 14 (Feb. 1983), 507–524.

38. Bureau of Municipal Research, *A Report on the Division of Child Hygiene, Department of Health* (New York: Bureau of Municipal Research, 1911), p. 16.

39. Aristotle, *Politics* transl. by Carnes Lord (Chicago: University of Chicago Press, 1984), book 1, chapter 2, p. 37.

40. See, for example, J. Maxwell Elden, "Political Efficacy at Work: The Connection between More Autonomous Forms of Workplace Organization and a More Participatory Politics," *American Political Science Review*, 75 (March 1981), 43–58 and Carole Pateman, *Participation and Democratic Theory* (Cambridge: Cambridge University Press, 1970).

41. Ernest Boyer, "Civic Education for Responsible Citizens," *Educational Leadership*, 48 (Nov. 1990), 4–7.

42. Steven Rosenstone and John Hansen, *Mobilization, Participation and Democracy in America* (New York: Macmillan, 1993), p. 14.

43. See the analysis in Richard Battistoni, *Public Schooling and the Education of Democratic Citizens* (Jackson, Mississippi: University Press of Mississippi, 1985), pp. 101–108.

44. John Godbold, "Oral Questioning Practices of Teachers in Social Studies Classes," *Educational Leadership*, 28 (October 1970), 61–67.

45. Illinois State Office of Education, *Illinois Inventory of Educational Progress* (Washington, D.C.: ERIC, Dec. 1980), cited in Battistoni, *Public Schooling*, p. 110.

46. Fred Newmann, "Citizenship Education in the United States: A Statement of Needs, " *National Civic Review*, 76 (July/August 1987), 280–287.

47. Boyer, "Civic Education for Responsible Citizens," p. 5.

48. Ralph Thayer, "The Local Government Annual Report as a Policy Planning Opportunity, " *Public Administration Review*, 38 (July/August 1978), 373–376.

49. George Rejda, *Social Insurance and Economic Security*, 5th ed. (Englewood Cliffs, N.J.: Prentice-Hall, 1994), p. 280.

50. See, for example, Bureau of Municipal Research, *Report of Investigations for the Associated Charities of Syracuse, New York* and *Administrative Methods of the City Government of Los Angeles, California* published by (New York: Bureau of Municipal Research, 1912) and (Los Angeles: Municipal League of Los Angeles, 1913), respectively.

51. See the discussion in John Forester, *Planning in the Face of Power* (Berkeley, California: University of California Press, 1989), p. 57.

52. Ralph Thayer, "The Local Government Annual Report . . ." and David Ammons, "Overcoming the Inadequacies of Performance Measurement in Local Government: The Case of Libraries and Leisure Services, " *Public Administration Review*, 55 (Jan./Feb. 1995), 37–47.

53. Reagen and Fedor-Thurman, "Public Participation . . ."

54. William Allen, "How May a Community Learn Its Unmet School Needs?" Unpublished address to National Education Association, Division of Superintendence, St. Louis Missouri, Feb. 27, 1912. Available New York Public Library.

55. See the discussion in Benjamin Barber, *Strong Democracy: Participatory Politics for a New Age* (Berkeley, California: University of California Press, 1984), p. 154.

Chapter 6

1. Donald Kettl, "Appraising the NPR: Executive Summary," *The Public Manager*, 23 (Fall 1994), 3–8.

2. Kenneth Langton and M. Kent Jennings, "Political Socialization and the High School Civics Curriculum in the United States, " *American Political Science Review*, 62 (Sept. 1968), 852–867 and Richard Niemi and Jane Junn, "Civics Courses and the Political Knowledge of High School Seniors," Unpublished paper prepared for the American Political Science Association Conference, Washington, D.C., Sept. 1993.

3. Paul Allen Beck and M. Kent Jennings, "Pathways to Participation," *American Political Science Review*, 76 (March 1982), 94–108.

4. See, for example, Benjamin Barber and Richard Battistoni, "A Season of Learning: Introducing Service Learning into the Liberal Arts

Curriculum," *PS: Political Science and Politics*, 26 (June 1993), 235–240, Alice Halsted and Joan Schine, "Service Learning: The Promise and the Risk" and Jodi Raybuck, "Lessons in the Common Good: Voluntarism on College Campuses," both in *New England Journal of Public Policy*, 10 (Summer 1994), 251–257 and 283–292, respectively.

5. Barber and Battistoni, "A Season of Learning . . ."

6. M. Kent Jennings and Richard Niemi, *Generations and Politics* (Princeton, N.J.: Princeton University Press, 1981).

7. The organization can be contacted at Brown University, Box 1975, Providence, Rhode Island.

8. See Raybuck, "Lessons in the Common Good . . ."

9. Richard Battistoni, "Education for Democracy: Service Learning and Pedagogical Reform in Higher Education," Unpublished paper prepared for the American Political Science Association Conference, New York City, Sept. 1994.

10. Ibid., p. 9.

11. New Jersey Institute of Technology, Office of Community and Public Service, *Service Learning Handbook* (Newark, N.J.: New Jersey Institute of Technology, 1993), p. 7.

12. James Chesney and Otto Feinstein, "Making Political Activity a Requirement in Introductory Political Science Courses, " *PS: Political Science and Politics*, 26, 3 (1993), 535–538.

13. Ernest Boyer, *High School: A Report on Secondary Education in America* (New York: Harper and Row, 1983), pp. 209–210.

14. Susan Schwartz, "Encouraging Youth Community Service: The Broadening Role of High Schools and Colleges," *National Civic Review*, 76 (July/August 1987), 288–301.

15. Boyer, *High School*, pp. 104–106.

16. Barber and Battistoni, "A Season of Service . . ." (quote on p. 237).

17. *Efficient Citizen*, 1 (Jan. 1914), p. 102.

18. See, for example, Jeffrey Abramson, F. Christopher Arterton and Gary Orren, *The Electronic Commonwealth* (New York: Basic Books, 1988), Brue Gates, "Knowledge, Networks and Neighborhoods: Will Microcomputers Make Us Better Citizens?" *Public Administration Review*,

44 (March 1984), special issue, 164–169, and Ithiel de Sola Pool (ed.), *Talking Back: Citizen Feedback and Cable Technology* (Cambridge, MA: MIT Press, 1973).

19. Harlan Cleveland, "The Twilight of Hierarchy: Speculations on the Global Information Society," *Public Administration Review*, 45 (Jan./Feb. 1985), 185–195 (quote on p. 194).

20. Walter Mossberg, "A Primer on Plugging You and Your PC Into the On-Line Trend," *Wall Street Journal* (Jan. 5, 1995), p. B1.

21. The strategy discussed here does not reach the homeless population and would not be efficacious with people who cannot or do not read.

22. See the analysis in William Knox, "Problems of Communication in Large Cities," in *Talking Back*, ed. by Ithiel de Sola Pool, pp. 103–114.

23. Executive Office of the President, National Performance Review, *From Red Tape to Results: Creating a Government that Works Better and Costs Less* (Washington, D.C.: U.S. Government Printing Office, 1993), p. 83.

24. David Ammons, "Overcoming the Inadequacies of Performance Measurement in Local Government: The Case of Libraries and Leisure Services," *Public Administration Review*, 55 (Jan./Feb. 1995), 37–47.

25. Benjamin Barber, *Strong Democracy* (Berkeley: University of California Press, 1984) and Stephen Elkin, *City and Regime in the American Republic* (Chicago: University of Chicago Press, 1987).

26. Barber, p. 271.

27. William Allen, "Reminiscences" (1949/1950), vol. 4, p. 525. Unpublished manuscript available in Oral History Collection, Columbia University.

28. Maria Newman, "Reports Tell Parents How Schools Perform," *New York Times* (Feb. 7, 1995), B2.

REFERENCES

I. Published Material

Abramson, Jeffrey, F. Christopher Arterton and Garry Orren. *The Electronic Commonwealth*. New York: Basic Books, 1988.

Abramson, Paul and John Aldrich. "The Decline of Electoral Participation in America," *American Political Science Review*, 76 (Sept. 1982), 502–521.

Allen, William. *Civics and Health*. Boston: Ginn and Co, 1909.

Allen, William. "Efficiency in City Government," *City Club Bulletin*, 2 (April 22, 1908), 127.

Allen, William. *Efficient Democracy*. New York: Dodd, Mead and Co, 1907.

Allen, William. "Instruction in Public Business," *Political Science Quarterly*, 22 (1908), 604–616.

Allen, William. "School Reports as They Are" in *School Progress and School Facts*. New York: Bureau of Municipal Research, 1909.

Allen, William. "The Budget Amendment of the Maryland Constitution," *National Municipal Review*, 6 (July 1917), 485–491.

Allen, William. *Universal Training for Citizenship and Public Service*. New York: Macmillan, 1917.

Allen, William. *Woman's Part in Government*. New York: Dodd, Mead and Co., 1911.

Amberg, Eda and William Allen. *Civic Lessons from Mayor Mitchel's Defeat*. New York: Institute for Public Service, 1921.

Ammons, David. "Overcoming the Inadequacies of Performance Measurement in Local Government: The Case of Libraries and Leisure Services," *Public Administration Review*, 55 (Jan./Feb.) 1995, 37–47.

Arendt, Hannah. *On Revolution*. New York: Viking, 1963.

Arendt, Hannah. *The Human Condition*. Chicago: University of Chicago Press, 1958.

Aristotle. *Politics*, transl. by Carnes Lord. Chicago: University of Chicago Press, 1984.

Austern, S. Ezra. "Surely, We Can Improve on Trial by Jury," *New York Times* (Dec. 31, 1994), 24.

Balfour, Danny and William Mesaros, "Connecting the Local Narratives: Public Administration as a Hermeneutic Science," *Public Administration Review*, 54 (Nov./Dec. 1994), 559–564.

Barber, Benjamin. *Strong Democracy: Participatory Politics for a New Age*. Berkeley, CA: University of California Press, 1984.

Barber, Benjamin and Richard Battistoni. "A Season of Learning: Introducing Service Learning into the Liberal Arts Curriculum," *PS: Political Science and Politics*, 26 (June 1993), 235–240.

Battistoni, Richard. *Public Schooling and the Education of Democratic Citizens*. Jackson, Miss.: University Press of Mississippi, 1985.

Beck, Paul Allen and M. Kent Jennings. "Pathways to Participation," *American Political Science Review*, 76 (March 1982), 94–108.

Boll, Heinrich. "The Man with the Knives" in *Great German Short Stories* ed. by Stephen Spender. New York: Dell, 1960.

Borgsdorf, Del. "The Local Citizen: Taxpayer, Voter and Customer" in *Effective Communication: A Local Government Guide* ed. by Kenneth Wheeler. Washington, D.C.: International City/County Management Association, 1995.

Boyer, Ernest. "Civic Education for Responsible Citizens," *Educational Leadership*, 48 (Nov. 1990), 4–7.

Boyer, Ernest. *High School: A Report on Secondary Education in America*. New York: Harper and Row, 1983.

———. "Bruere, A Chicago Don Quixote," *Tammany Times* (Feb. 13, 1909), 9.

Bruere, Henry. "America's Unemployment Problem," *Annals*, 61 (Sept. 1915), 11–23.

Bruere, Henry. "Efficiency in City Government." *Annals*, 41 (May 1912), 1–22.

Bruere, Henry. "Public Utilities Regulation in New York." *Annals*, 31 (May 1908), 535–551.

Bruere, Henry. "The Future of the Police Arm from an Engineering Standpoint," *American Society of Mechanical Engineers Transactions*, 36 (1914), 535–547.

Bruere, Henry. *The New City Government*. New York: D. Appleton and Co, 1912.

Bureau of City Betterment. *The Police Problem in New York City*. New York: Citizens Union, 1906.

Bureau of Municipal Research. *A Report on the Division of Child Hygiene, Department of Health*. New York: Bureau of Municipal Research, 1911.

Bureau of Municipal Research. "A Report on the Homes and Family Budgets of 100 Patrolmen," in *Police in America*. New York: Arno Press and *New York Times*, 1971.

Bureau of Municipal Research. *Administrative Methods of the City Government of Los Angeles, California*. Los Angeles: Municipal League of Los Angeles, 1913.

Bureau of Municipal Research. *Business Methods of New York City's Police Department*. New York: Bureau of Municipal Research, 1909.

Bureau of Municipal Research. *Digest of the School Inquiry*. New York: Bureau of Municipal Research, 1913.

Bureau of Municipal Research. *Help-Your-School Surveys*. New York: Bureau of Municipal Research, 1913.

Bureau of Municipal Research. *Making a Municipal Budget*. New York: Bureau of Municipal Research, 1907.

Bureau of Municipal Research. *Purposes and Methods of the Bureau of Municipal Research*. New York: Bureau of Municipal Research, 1907.

Bureau of Municipal Research. *Report of Investigations for the Associated Charities of Syracuse, New York*. New York: Bureau of Municipal Research, 1912.

Bureau of Municipal Research. *Report on a Survey of the Department of Public Safety, Pittsburgh.* New York: Bureau of Municipal Research, 1913.

Bureau of Municipal Research and Training School for Public Service. *Efficiency and Next Needs of St. Paul's Health Department.* New York: Bureau of Municipal Research, 1913.

Burks, Jesse. "Efficiency Standards in Municipal Management." *National Municipal Review*, 1 (July 1912), 364–371.

Burtt, Shelley. "The Politics of Virtue Today: A Critique and a Proposal." *American Political Science Review*, 87, (June 1993), 360–368.

Callahan, Raymond. *Education and the Cult of Efficiency.* Chicago: University of Chicago Press, 1962.

Capes, William. *The Modern City and Its Government.* New York: E. P. Dutton, 1922.

Cerf, Myrtile. "Bureaus of Public Efficiency." *National Municipal Review*, 2 (July 1913), 39–47.

Chesney, James and Otto Feinstein. "Making Political Activity a Requirement in Introductory Political Science Courses." *PS: Political Science and Politics*, XXVI (September 1993), 535–538.

Cleveland, Frederick. *Chapters on Municipal Administration and Accounting.* New York: Longmans, Green and Co, 1909.

Cleveland, Frederick. *Organized Democracy.* New York: Longmans, Green and Co, 1913.

Cleveland, Frederick. "Municipal Ownership as a Form of Governmental Control," *Annals*, 35 (1906), 359–370.

Cleveland, Frederick. "The Need for Coordinating Municipal, State and National Activities," *Annals*, 41 (May 1912), 25–39.

Cleveland, Harlan. "The Twilight of Hierarchy: Speculations on the Global Information Society," *Public Administration Review*, 45 (Jan./Feb. 1985), 185–195.

Cole, Richard and David Caputo. "The Public Hearing as an Effective Citizen Participation Mechanism," *American Political Science Review*, 78 (June 1984), 404–416.

Cooper, Terry. "Citizenship and Professionalism in Public Administration," *Public Administration Review*, 44, special issue (March 1984), 143–149.

Critchlow, Donald. *The Brookings Institution, 1916–1952: Expertise and the Public Interest in a Democratic Society*. DeKalb, Illinois: Northern Illinois University Press, 1985.

Dahl, Robert. *Modern Political Analysis*. Englewood Cliffs, New Jersey: Prentice-Hall, 1963.

Dahl, Robert. *Who Governs?* New Haven, CT: Yale University Press, 1960.

Dahlberg, Jane. *The New York Bureau of Municipal Research*. New York: New York University Press, 1966.

Denhardt, Robert. *The Pursuit of Significance: Strategies for Managerial Success*. Belmont, CA: Wadsworth, 1993.

DiIulio, John, Jr, Gerald Garvey, and Donald Kettl. *Improving Government Performance: An Owner's Manual*. Washington, D.C.: Brookings, 1993.

———. "Directors Fall Out in Research Bureau." *New York Times* (July 18, 1914), 14.

———. "Dr. Allen Attacked by Research Chief." *New York Times* (Feb. 4, 1915), 7.

Drost, Walter. *David Snedden and Education for Social Efficiency*. Madison, WI: University of Wisconsin Press, 1967.

Edelman, Murray. *The Symbolic Uses of Politics*. Urbana: University of Illinois Press, 1985.

Efficient Citizen, 1913–1914.

Efficient Citizenship, 1908–1913.

Eldon, J. Maxwell. "Political Efficacy at Work: The Connection between More Autonomous Forms of Workplace Organization and a More Participatory Politics," *American Political Science Review*, 75 (March 1981), 43–58.

Eliot, Charles. "City Government By Fewer Men." In *Charles W. Eliot: The Man and His Beliefs* ed. William Neilson. New York: Harper and Brothers, 1926.

Elkin, Stephen. *City and Regime in the American Republic*. Chicago: University of Chicago Press, 1987.

Emerson, Harrington. *Efficiency as a Basis for Operations and Wages*. New York: Engineering Magazine Press, 1912.

Emerson, Harrington. *Twelve Principles of Efficiency*. New York: Engineering Magazine Press, 1912.

Euben, J. Peter. "Democracy Ancient and Modern," *PS: Political Science and Politics*, 26 (Sept. 1993), 478–481.

Executive Office of the President, National Performance Review. *From Red Tape to Results: Creating a Government That Works Better and Costs Less*. Washington, D.C.: U.S. Government Printing Office, 1993.

Executive Office of the President, National Performance Review. *Putting Customers First: Standards for Serving the American People*. Washington, D.C.: U.S. Government Printing Office, 1994.

Fayol, Henri. *General and Industrial Management*, trans. C. Storrs. London: Sir Isaac Pittman, 1949.

Fitzpatrick, Edward. "What is Civic Education?" *National Municipal Review*, 5 (April 1916), 278–282.

Forester, John. *Planning in the Face of Power*. Berkeley: University of California Press, 1989.

Frederickson, H. George. "The Seven Principles of Total Quality Politics . . ." *Public Administration Times*, 17, 1 (1993), 9.

Gates, Bruce. "Knowledge, Networks and Neighborhoods: Will Microcomputers Make Us Better Citizens?" *Public Administration Review*, 44, special issue (March 1984), 164–169.

Gawthrop, Louis. "Civis, Civitas, and Civilitas: A New Focus for the Year 2000," *Public Administration Review*, 44, special issue (March 1984), 101–107.

Gerstner, Louis, Jr. et al. *Reinventing Education: Entrepeneurship in America's Public Schools*. New York: Dutton, 1994.

Godbold, John. "Oral Questioning Practices of Teachers in Social Studies Classes," *Educational Leadership*, 28 (Oct. 1970), 61–67.

Golembiewski, Robert. "A Critique of "Democratic Administration" and Its Supporting Ideation," *American Political Science Review*, 66 (Dec. 1977), 1488–1507.

Goodnow, Frank and Frederic Howe. "The Organization, Status and Procedure of the Department of Education, City of New York." In *Report of Committee on School Inquiry*. New York: Board of Estimate and Apportionment, 1912.

Goodsell, Charles. "Charles A. Beard, Prophet for Public Administration," *Public Administration Review*, 46 (Mar./Apr. 1986), 105–107.

Goodsell, Charles. *The Case for Bureaucracy*, 2nd ed. Chatham: New Jersey: Chatham House, 1985.

Goodsell, Charles. "The Grace Commission: Seeking Efficiency for the Whole People?" *Public Administration Review*, 44 (May/June 1984), 196–204.

Gordon, George. *Public Administration in America*, 3rd ed. New York: St. Martin's Press, 1986.

Gore, Al., Jr. "The New Job of the Federal Executive." *Public Administration Review*, 54 (July/August 1994), 317–321.

Graham, George. *Education for Public Administration*. Chicago: Public Administration Service, 1941.

Gulick, Luther. *The National Institute of Public Administration*. New York: National Institute of Public Administration, 1928.

Gulick, Luther and Lyndall Urwick, eds. *Papers on the Science of Administration*. New York: Institute of Public Administration, 1937.

Halstad, Alice and Joan Schine. "Service Learning: The Promise and the Risk," *New England Journal of Public Policy*, 10 (Summer 1994), 251–257.

Hanus, Paul. *Adventuring in Education*. Cambridge, MA: Harvard University Press, 1937.

Hanus, Paul. *School Efficiency: A Constructive Study Applied to New York City*. Yonkers, New York: World Book Co., 1913.

Harwood Group. *Citizens and Politics: A View from Main Street America*. Dayton, Ohio: Kettering Foundation, 1991.

Henry, Nicholas. *Public Administration and Public Affairs*, 4th ed. Englewood Cliffs, New Jersey: Prentice-Hall, 1988.

Hofstadter, Richard. *The Age of Reform*. New York: Alfred Knopf, 1959.

Howe, Frederic. *The Modern City and Its Problems*. New York: Scribner's, 1915.

Jennings, M. Kent and Richard Niemi. *Generations and Politics*. Princeton, N.J.: Princeton University Press, 1981.

Kettl, Donald. "Appraising the NPR: Executive Summary," *The Public Manager*, 23 (Fall 1994), 3–8.

Knox, William. "Problems of Communication in Large Cities." In *Talking Back: Citizen Feedback and Cable Technology*, ed. I. de Sola Pool. Cambridge, MA: MIT Press, 1973.

Korten, David. *Getting to the 21st Century: Voluntary Action and the Global Agenda*. West Hartford, CT: Kumarian Press, 1990.

Kweit, Mary and Robert Kweit. "The Politics of Policy Analysis: The Role of Citizen Participation in Analytic Decision Making." In *Citizen Participation in Public Decision Making*, ed. J. DeSario and S. Langton. Westport, CT: Greenwood, 1987.

Lakoff, George and Mark Johnson. *Metaphors We Live By*. Chicago: University of Chicago Press, 1980.

Landau, Martin. "On the Use of Metaphor in Political Analysis," *Social Research*, 28 (Autumn 1961), 331–353.

Langton, Kenneth and M. Kent Jennings. "Political Socialization and the High School Civics Curriculum in the United States," *American Political Science Review*, 62 (Sept. 1968), 852–867.

Light, Paul. "Partial Quality Management," *Government Executive*, 26 (April 1994), 65–66.

Lueck, Thomas. "Business Districts Grow at Price of Accountability," *New York Times* (Nov. 20, 1994), 1 and 46.

Lyons, W. and David Lowery. "Governmental Fragmentation Versus Consolidation," *Public Administration Review*, 49 (Nov./Dec. 1989), 533–543.

MacNair, Ray, Russell Caldwell, and Leonard Pollane. "Citizen Participation in Public Bureaucracies: Foul-Weather Friends," *Administration and Society*, 14 (Feb. 1983), 507–524.

Mani, Bonnie. "Old Wine in New Bottles Tastes Better: A Case Study of TQM Implementation in the IRS," *Public Administration Review*, 55 (March/April 1995), 147–158.

Mayers, Lewis. "The New York School Inquiry," *National Municipal Review*, 3 (April 1914), 327–339.

McGregor, Eugene, Jr. "The Great Paradox of Democratic Citizenship and Public Personnel Administration." *Public Administration Review*, 44, special issue (March 1984), 126–132.

Metz, Herman. *The Cost of Government of the City of New York with an Analysis of the Budget of the Year 1909*. New York: Finance Department, 1909.

Miller, Eugene. "Metaphor and Political Knowledge," *American Political Science Review*, 73 (March 1979), 155–170.

Moe, Ronald. "The "Reinventing Government" Exercise: Misinterpreting the Problem, Misjudging the Consequences," *Public Administration Review* 54 (March/April 1994), 111–122.

Moore, Ernest. *How New York City Administers Its Schools*. Yonkers, New York: World Book Co., 1913.

Mosher, Frederick. *Democracy and the Public Service*. New York: Oxford University Press, 1968.

Mossberg, Walter. "A Primer on Plugging You and Your PC Into the On-Line Trend," *Wall Street Journal* (Jan. 5 1995), B1.

Municipal Research, 1913–1914. Available at Institute of Public Administration, New York.

———. "Municipal Research," *New York Times* (July 20, 1914), 6.

Munro, William. *Principles and Methods of Municipal Administration*. New York: Macmillan, 1915.

New Jersey Institute of Technology, Service Corps. *Service Learning Handbook*, revised ed. Newark: N.J.: New Jersey Institute of Technology, 1993.

New York City Board of Education. *Journal of the Board of Education of the City of New York*. New York: Board of Education, 1904.

New York City Board of Estimate and Apportionment, Committee on School Inquiry. *Report of Committee on School Inquiry*. New York: Board of Estimate and Apportionment, 1911–1913.

New York City Finance Department. *Cost of Government of the City of New York*. New York: Finance Department, 1908.

———. "New York School Inquiry," *National Municipal Review*, 2 (Jan. 1913), 88–93.

———. "New York's Budget Exhibit," *Charities and the Commons*, 21 (Oct. 10, 1908), 74.

Newman, Maria. "Reports Tell Parents How Schools Perform," *New York Times* (Feb. 7, 1995), B2.

Newmann, Fred. "Citizenship Education in the United States: A Statement of Needs," *National Civic Review*, 76 (July/Aug 1987), 280–287.

Nigro, Felix and Lloyd Nigro. *Modern Public Administration*, 7th ed. New York: Harper and Row, 1989.

———. "Not Moved by Rockefeller," *New York Times* (July 19, 1914), sec. II, p. 8.

Osborne, David and Ted Gaebler. *Reinventing Government: How the Entrepeneurial Spirit is TransForming the Public Sector from Schoolhouse to State House, City Hall to Pentagon.* Reading, MA: Addison-Wesley, 1992.

Ostrom, Vincent. *The Intellectual Crisis in American Public Administration.* University Ala.: University of Alabama Press, 1974.

Parker, Franklin. "Abraham Flexner, 1866–1959," *History of Education Quarterly*, 2 (Dec. 1962), 199–209.

Pateman, Carole. *Participation and Democratic Theory.* Cambridge: Cambridge University Press, 1970.

Poister, Theodore and Gary Henry. "Citizen Ratings of Public and Private Service Quality: A Comparative Perspective," *Public Administration Review*, 54 (March/April 1994), 155–160.

Pool, Ithiel de Sola, ed. *Talking Back: Citizen Feedback and Cable Technology.* Cambridge, MA: MIT Press, 1973.

Posner, Richard. "Juries on Trial," *Commentary*, 99 (March 1995), 49–52.

Prendergast, William. "Efficiency through Accounting," *Annals*, 41 (May 1912), 43–56.

Ravitch, Diane. *The Great School Wars, New York City, 1805–1973.* New York: Basic Books, 1974.

Raybuck, Jodi. "Lessons in the Common Good: Voluntarism on College Campuses, " *New England Journal of Public Policy*, 10 (Summer 1994), 251–257.

Reagen, Michael and Lynn Fedor-Thurman. "Public Participation: Reflections on the California Energy Policy Experience," in *Citizen Participation in Public Decision Making*, ed. by Jack DeSario and Stuart Langton. Westport, CT: Greenwood Press, 1987.

Rejda, George. *Social Insurance and Economic Security*, 5th ed. Englewood Cliffs, N.J.: Prentice-Hall, 1994.

Roberts, Alasdair. "Demonstrating Neutrality: The Rockefeller Philanthropies and the Evolution of Public Administration," *Public Administration Review*, 54 (May/June 1994), 221–228.

Rosenbloom, David. "Have an Administrative Rx? Don't Forget the Politics." *Public Administration Review*, 53 (November/December 1993), 503–507.

Rosenbloom, David. *Public Administration*, 2nd ed. New York: Random House, 1989.

Rosener, Judy. "Making Bureaucracy Responsive: A Study of the Impact of Citizen Participation and Staff Recommendations on Regulatory Decision Making," *Public Administration Review*, 42 (July/Aug. 1982), 339–345.

Rosenstone, Steven and John Hansen. *Mobilization, Participation and Democracy in America*. New York: Macmillan, 1993.

Rowe, Leo. *Problems of City Government*. New York: D. Appleton and Co, 1908.

Rubin, Irene. "Early Budget Reformers: Democracy, Efficiency and Budget Reforms," *American Review of Public Administration*, 24 (Sept. 1994), 229–251.

Ryan, Lori Verstegen and William Scott. "Ethics and Organizational Reflection: The Rockefeller Foundation and Postwar "Moral Deficits," 1942–1954," *Academy of Management Review*, 20 (April 1995), 438–461.

Sait, Edward. "Research and Reference Bureaus," *National Municipal Review*, 2 (Jan. 1913), 48–56.

Sayre, Wallace and Herbert Kaufman. *Governing New York City*. New York: Russell Sage, 1960.

Schachter, Hindy Lauer. "Graduate Education in Public Administration: The Introductory Course," *International Journal of Public Administration*, 16, 1 (1993), 1–13.

Schachter, Hindy Lauer. "The Role of Efficiency in Bureaucratic Study, " in *Handbook of Bureuacracy*, ed. by Ali Farazmand. New York: Marcel Dekker, 1994.

Schiesl, Martin. *The Politics of Efficiency*. Berkeley, California: University of California Press, 1977.

Schwartz, Susan. "Encouraging Youth Community Service: The Broadening Role of High Schools and Colleges," *National Civic Review*, 76 (July/Aug. 1987), 288–301.

Shafritz, Jay and Albert Hyde. *Classics of Public Administration*, 2nd ed. Chicago: Dorsey, 1987.

Simon, Herbert. *Administrative Behavior*. New York: Free Press, 1947.

Snedden, David and William Allen. *School Reports and School Efficiency*. New York: Macmillan, 1908.

Starling, Grover. *Managing the Public Sector*, 3rd ed. Chicago: Dorsey, 1986.

Stillman, Richard, II. *Public Administration: Concepts and Cases*, 4th ed. Boston: Houghton Mifflin, 1988.

Stivers, Camilla. "Settlement Women and Bureau Men: Constructing a Usable Past for Public Administration." *Public Administration Review*, 55 (Nov./Dec. 1995), 522–529.

Stivers, Camilla. "The Public Agency as Polis: Active Citizenship in the Administrative State." *Administration and Society*, 22 (May 1990), 86–105.

Stone, Alice and Donald Stone. "Early Development of Education in Public Administration" in *American Public Administration: Past, Present, Future*, ed. Frederick Mosher. University, Alabama: University of Alabama Press, 1975.

Swiss, James. "Adapting Total Quality Management (TQM) to Government," *Public Administration Review*, 52 (July/August, 1992), 356–362.

Taylor, Frederick. *Shop Management*. New York: Harper and Brothers, 1947 (originally 1903).

Thayer, Ralph. "The Local Government Annual Report as a Policy Planning Opportunity," *Public Administration Review*, 38 (July/August 1978), 373–376.

Thompson, James and Vernon Jones, "Reinventing the Federal Government: The Role of Theory in Reform Implementation," *American Review of Public Administration*, 25 (June 1995), 183–199.

Tildsley, John. "School Reports as They Are: A Rejoinder" in *School Progress and School Facts*. New York: Bureau of Municipal Research, 1909.

Toulmin, Stephen. *Human Understanding.* Princeton, N.J.: Princeton University Press, 1972.

Tyack, David and Elizabeth Hansot. *Managers of Virtue.* New York: Basic Books, 1982.

United States President's Commission on Economy and Efficiency. *Message of the President of the United States on Economy and Efficiency in the Government Service.* Washington, D.C.: U.S. Government Printing Office, 1912.

United States President's Committee on Administrative Management. *Report of the Committee with Studies of Administrative Management in the Federal Government.* Washington, D.C.: U.S. Government Printing Office, 1937.

Upson, Lent. "The Value of Municipal Exhibits," *National Municipal Review*, 4 (Jan. 1915), 65–69.

Van Riper, Paul. "Luther Gulick on Frederick Taylor and Scientific Management," *Journal of Management History*, 1 (1995), 7–9.

Verba, Sidney et al. "Citizen Activity: Who Participates? What Do They Say?" *American Political Science Review*, 87 (June 1993), 303–318.

Waldo, Dwight. "Response," *Public Administration Review*, 44, special issue (March 1984), 107–109.

Waldo, Dwight. *The Administrative State.* New York: Ronald Press, 1948.

White, Leonard. *Trends in Public Administration.* New York: McGraw Hill, 1933.

Wiebe, Robert. *The Search for Order, 1877–1920.* New York: Hill and Wang, 1967.

Willoughby, W.F. *Principles of Public Administration with Special Reference to the National and State Governments of the United States.* Baltimore: Johns Hopkins, 1927.

Wirt, Frederick and Michael Kirst. *Schools in Conflict.* Berkeley, Calif.: McCutcheon, 1982.

Wolin, Sheldon, "Democracy: Electoral and Athenian," *PS: Political Science and Politics*, 26 (Sept. 1993), 475–477.

II. Unpublished Material

Papers, Reports, and Reminiscences

Allen, William. "How May a Community Learn Its Unmet School Needs?" Paper presented at the National Education Association Conference, St. Louis, Feb. 27, 1912 (New York Public Library).

Allen, William. "Reasons Why Mr. Allen Believes that Mr. Rockefeller's Conditional Offer of Support to the New York Bureau of Municipal Research Should Not Be Accepted." Remarks to BMR Board of Trustees, May, 11, 1914 (New York Public Library).

Allen, William. "Reminiscences," 1949/1950 (Oral History Collection, Columbia University).

Association for Improving the Condition of the Poor. "Communication on Behalf of Vacation and Night Schools, Recreation Centers and Popular Lectures," June 1905 (New York Public Library).

Battistoni, Richard. "Education for Democracy: Service Learning and Pedagogical Reform in Higher Education." Paper presented at the American Political Science Association Conference, New York City, August 1994.

Beard, Charles. "Philosophy, Science and Art of Public Administration." Paper presented at the Governmental Research Association, Princeton, Sept. 8, 1939 (New York Public Library).

Binkerd, Robert. "Reminiscences," April/May 1949 (Oral History Collection, Columbia University).

Cleveland, Frederick. "Work to Be Done by Institute for Municipal Research," Feb. 1905 (Citizens Union Papers, Manuscript Collection, Columbia University).

Cutting, R. Fulton. "Regarding the Educational Activities of the Bureau of Municipal Research and Training School for Public Service," April 4, 1914 (Rockefeller Archives).

Flexner, Abraham. "The Educational Activities of the Bureau of Municipal Research of New York: A Report to the General Education Board," 1914 (Rockefeller Archives).

Laity League, Social Service Conference. "Honesty, Economy, Efficiency," election pamphlet, 1913 (Citizens Union Papers, Manuscript Collection, Columbia University).

Lane, Larry and Gary Marshall. "Reinventing OPM: Adventures, Issues, and Implications." Paper presented at the American Society for Public Administration Conference, San Antonio, July, 1995.

Niemi, Richard and Jane Junn. "Civic Courses and the Political Knowledge of High School Seniors." Paper presented at the American Political Science Association Conference, Washington, D.C., Sept. 1993.

Prendergast, William. "Reminiscences," 1948–1951 (Oral History Collection, Columbia University).

————. "Report No. 2 of the Special Committee of Five," 1904 (Special Collections, Teachers College, Columbia University).

Letters and Memoranda

Allen, William letters to 1) Abraham Flexner, May 5, 1913, Feb. 5, 1914; 2) John D. Rockefeller, Jr., May 9, 1913, June 19, 1913, Jan. 17, 1918, June 29, 1925.

Cleveland, Frederick letters to 1) Abraham Flexner, May 28, 1915; 2) Jerome Greene, Oct. 8, 1914; 3) the Industrial Relations Commission, Feb. 2, 1915.

Cutting, R. Fulton letters to 1) Jerome Greene, Nov. 24, 1914; 2) Starr Murphy, April 7, 1916.

Eliot, Charles letter to Jerome Greene, Nov. 15, 1912.

Flexner, Abraham letters to 1)Wallace Buttrick, April 10, 1914; 2) B. Tinker, Jan. 19, 1914; and memorandum, Feb. 4, 1915.

Fosdick, Raymond letter to W. S. Learned, Jan. 30, 1923.

Greene, Jerome letters to 1) William Allen, Oct. 9, 1913; 2) Paul Hanus, Nov. 11, 1912, March 13, 1913; 3) Charles Howland, April 16, 1913; 4) Charles Moore, March 10, 1913; and memoranda on 1) a letter from William Allen, Nov. 13, 1912; 2) the BMR, March 17, 1913.

Hanus, Paul letters to 1) Abraham Flexner, Dec. 23, 1913; 2) Jerome Greene, Nov. 12, 1912, March 12, 1913 and memorandum, June 15, 1913.

Mandel, Edward letter to William Allen, Jan. 19, 1914.

Maxwell, William letter to Abraham Flexner, Dec. 11, 1913.

————. "Memorandum of Correspondence between Dr. Allen of the Bureau of Municipal Research and Mr. John D. Rockefeller, Jr.

Regarding Investigation of the Educational Work of the Bureau of Municipal Research," n.d.

Moore, Ernest letter to Jerome Greene, Nov. 19, 1912.

Murphy, Starr letters to 1) William Allen, Nov. 29, 1912; 2) R. Fulton Cutting, April 18, 1916; 3)John D. Rockefeller, Jr., May 18, 1911; 4) John D. Rockefeller, Jr. or Sr. (not specified), Feb. 16, 1914.

Pritchett, Henry letter to Abraham Flexner, April 10, 1914.

Rockefeller, John Jr. letters to 1) Charles Coffin, Aug. 7, 1914; 2) Abraham Flexner, May 9, 1913; 3) John D. Rockefeller, Sr., Jan. 7, 1909.

Tinker, B. letter to H. L. Brittain, May 6, 1913.

INDEX

ABC powers, 20
Active citizenship. *See* efficient
    citizenship and owner model of
    citizenship
Advisory Commission on Financial
    Administration and Accounting, 20
Allen, William Henry: background, 17,
    22; and Bureau of Municipal
    Research incorporation, 19–20; and
    citizen interest in public affairs, 68;
    and class, 39–42; and education for
    citizenship, 35; and *Efficient
    Citizenship*, 37; and Abraham
    Flexner, 49–50; and Paul Hanus, 45;
    and information, 18–19, 22, 32–35,
    88; and the Institute of Public
    Service, 53–54, 69; on the Maryland
    constitution, 53; and William
    Maxwell, 18; personality, 21; on
    public-administration training,
    27–28; resignation from the Bureau
    of Municipal Research, 52; and the
    Rockefellers, 51–54; and the school
    budget controversy, 18–19; and the
    school survey, 45–47; social work
    experience, 17–18. *See also* Bureau
    of Municipal Research; efficient
    citizenship; owner model of
    citizenship
American Political Science
    Association, 28

Arendt, Hannah, 14
Aristotle, 71
Association for Improving the
    Condition of the Poor, 18, 20

Bachman, Frank, 50
Barber, Benjamin, 14, 86
Bingham, Theodore, 24, 28
Binkerd, Robert, 21
Board of Education: and the
    Association for Improving the
    Condition of the Poor, 18; and the
    budget controversy of 1904, 18–19;
    finance committee of, 37; models
    for, 43–44; Ernest Moore's report
    on, 44–47
Board of Estimate and Apportionment,
    23; and the school survey, 43, 47
Boyer, Ernest, 74, 82
Bruere, Henry, 24; and the Bureau of
    City Betterment, 20; and class, 41;
    as Bureau of Municipal Research
    director, 20–21; as city
    chamberlain, 21; and education for
    citizenship, 35; and efficiency, 26,
    34; and information, 61; and police
    work, 22; and the school survey,
    43, 49. *See also* Bureau of
    Municipal Research and efficient
    citizenship
Bureau of City Betterment, 20

135

Bureau of Municipal Research, 4, 7, 10–16, 17; and budget exhibits, 36; and city budgets, 24; and class, 38–42; and economy, 25–27; and efficient citizenship, 31–42, 64, 70; and efficiency, 26; funding 22–23; and gender, 38–39; and information, 75; incorporation of, 20; optimism of, 71; and public-administration training, 27–29; and public hearings, 24, 75; reorganization of, 52, 54; and the school survey, 43–48; and scientific management, 23–24, 26, 28; and state public-service commissions, 15, 45; structure of, 20–21. *See also* Allen, William Henry; Bruere, Henry; Cleveland, Frederick; efficient citizenship; *Efficient Citizenship*, owner model of citizenship

Campus Compact, 79
Carnegie, Andrew, 20–22
Carnegie Foundation, 50
Carnegie Foundation for the Advancement of Teaching, 49, 74, 81
Churchill, Thomas, 47
Citizens Union, 20, 21
Citizenship, models of. *See* customer model of citizenship and owner model of citizenship
Civic Federation, 19
Cleveland, Frederick: background, 19, 22; on Bureau of Municipal Research incorporation, 19–20; as chair of the Commission on Economy and Efficiency, 21, 51–52; on citizen action, 62; on efficient citizenship, 31; and information, 24, 33; on the Maryland constitution, 53; on public hearings, 24; and the reorganization of the bureau, 51–52; and the school budget controversy, 19, 50; as sole director of the Bureau of Municipal

Research, 52–53. *See also* Bureau of Municipal Research and efficient citizenship
Columbia University, 27
Cortines, Ramon, 89
Commission on Economy and Efficiency, 2, 21
Committee on Administrative Management, 2
Customer model of citizenship, 1, 7–10, 57–60; and action, 61; and community, 63–65. *See also* reinventing government and National Performance Review Task Force
Cutting, R. Fulton: and Bureau of Municipal Research incorporation, 20–22; and the Flexner report, 50–51; after the reorganization of the bureau, 52

Dahlberg, Jane, 7

Education for citizenship, 72–74, 78–82
Efficient Citizen, 82
Efficient Citizenship, 10, 37–38; and the school survey, 47–49; and vulgarity, 50, 85
Efficient citizenship: citations to, 4; and contemporary American reality, 65–67; as customer-model alternative, 7; and education, 35; and inclusiveness, 38–42; and information, 32–33, 61; rise and fall of, 10–16, 54; strategies for, 31–32. *See also* Bureau of Munciipal Research and owner model of citizenship
Electronic communication, 82–84
Eliot Charles, 44; on the Bureau of Municipal Research, 47–48
Emerson, Harrington, 3, 28

Fayol, Henri, 3
Flexner, Abraham, 49–50, 52

Frederickson, George, 8, 14
Freedom of Information Act, 74

Gaebler, Ted, 7, 54, 61
Gawthrop, Louis, 62, 69
General Education Board, 46, 49
Gilbreth, Frank, 28
Gilbreth, Lillian, 28
Goodnow, Frank, 47
Gore, Al, Jr., 2, 6–7
Grace Commission, 2, 61
Greene, Jerome, 46–47, 52; on William
    Allen, 48–49
Grout, Edward, 18
Gulick, Luther, 3, 5, 6

Hanus, Paul, 43–44; and William
    Allen, 45–46; and the Bureau of
    Municipal Research, 47; and
    Abraham Flexner, 50; and John
    Mitchel, 46
Harriman family, 28
Harvard Law School, 21
Harvard University, 44
Haskins and Sells, 19
Howe, Frederick, 47

Institute of Municipal Research, 19, 22
Institute of Public Service, 53–54, 69
International City/County
    Management Association, 7
Italian Educational Alliance, 19

Jargon, 75
Jury duty, 66–67

Kettering Foundation study, 66, 80, 82
King, James, 58
Korten, David, 64

Maxwell, William, 18, 24; and bureau
    criticisms, 33–34
McGregor, Eugene, 62, 69
Metaphors, 7–10, 55, 60
Metz, Herman, 24, 28
Miller, Cyrus, 43

Mitchel, John Purroy, 21, 41; and the
    school survey, 43, 46
Moore, Ernest, 44, 46–47
Municipal League of Los Angeles, 33
Murphy, Starr, 22, 48, 50, 52

National Community Trust Act, 80
National Performance Review Task
    Force, 7–8, 27, 54, 89–90; and
    annual reports, 84; and community,
    64; goals of 58; and politics, 59–60;
    and the public-administration
    community, 2. See also customer
    model of citizenship and
    reinventing government
New Jersey Institute of Technology, 80
New Jersey State Charities Aid
    Association, 17
New York Association for Improving
    the Condition of the Poor. See
    Association for Improving the
    Condition of the Poor
New York Bureau of Municipal
    Research. See Bureau of Municipal
    Research
New York City Board of Education. See
    Board of Education
New York City Board of Estimate and
    Apportionment. See Board of
    Estimate and Apportionment
New York Times, 52

Osborne, David, 7, 54, 61
Ostrom, Vincent, 6
Owner model of citizenship, 1, 9–10,
    14, 31–42, 56–57; and action,
    61–62; arguments against, 67–72;
    and community, 63–65, 68;
    education for, 72–74, 78–82; and
    information, 74–76, 82–89. See also
    efficient citizenship

Papers on the Science of
    Administration, 5
Performance measures for local
    governments, 85–88

Prendergast, William, 21, 43, 68
President's Private Sector Survey on Cost Control, 61
Principles literature in public administration, 3–6
Pritchett, Henry, 50
Progressive movement, 3, 15, 24, 25, 43
Public administration: extrinsic reasons for change, 11–12; and funding sources, 12; growth as a field of inquiry, 2–3, 11, 13–14; intrinsic reasons for change, 11–12; principles of, 3–6

Reinventing government, 1, 7, 55; and economy, 27; strategies for, 77. *See also* customer model of citizenship; Gaebler, Ted; National Performance Review Task Force; Osborne, David
Reporting system for local government, 85–89
Roberts, Alasdair, 12–13
Rockefeller Foundation, 12
Rockefeller interests. *See* efficient citizenship, rise and fall of; Flexner, Abraham; Greene, Jerome; Rockefeller, John, Jr.; Rockefeller, John, Sr.
Rockefeller, John, Jr., 22, 49–50, 52–53
Rockefeller, John, Sr., 12, 20–22, 42, 48, 51
Roosevelt, Theodore, 41
Rubin, Irene, 51
Rutgers University, 80

School governance: economic model, 8; New York City system, 44; Progressive model, 43–44

School Review, 37
Scientific Management. *See* Bureau of Municipal Research and scientific management and Taylor, Frederick
Securities and Exchange Commission, 84
Service learning, 79–82
Simon, Herbert, 5
Social context of scientific inquiry, 11–12
Stivers, Camilla, 66
Syracuse University, 28

Taft, William Howard, 2, 21, 51, 89
Tammany Hall, 24, 36
Taylor, Frederick, 3, 5–6; influence on the Bureau of Municipal Research, 17, 23, 28, 45
Tildsley, John, 34
Total Quality Management (TQM), 8, 57–58
Toulmin, Stephen, 11–12

United States Commissions on Efficiency. *See* Commission on Economy and Efficiency; Committee on Administrative Management; Grace Commission; National Performance Review Task Force
University of Chicago, 17
University of Pennsylvania, 17, 19, 21
Urwick, Lyndall, 3, 5–6

Waldo, Dwight, 62
Wayne State University, 81